www.ingramcontent.com/pod-product-compliance
Lightning Source LLC
Chambersburg PA
CBHW042017150426
43197CB00002B/50

Dear Reader

The objective of Kendo World is to disseminate information that will help the international community of kendo aficionados in their study of the perennial path of traditional Japanese swordsmanship and related arts. Your purchase of this publication helps the Kendo World team travel around Japan to interview famous sensei, cover important kendo events, and pay translators for their tireless work deciphering kendo wisdom. We appreciate your continued support of Kendo World's aims to promote the beautiful art of kendo. If you are reading this publication on anything other than one of our authorised digital platforms (e.g. ZINIO, Kindle, iBooks), or in "Print on Demand" paper form via Amazon, then you are in possession of pirated material. As fellow kenshi, we appeal to your conscience in the hope that you refuse to participate in illegal file sharing of our copyrighted material. We agree that information belongs to everybody, but spare a thought for the time, effort, and resources that are required to bring it to you. Pirating is stealing. Without your backing, Kendo World will die. We don't want to die yet because there is still so much to do…

Happy reading and thank you.

Kendo World Team

Carbon Shinai
カーボンシナイ

- CF-Type
- DB-Type
- K1-Type
- K2-Type

Orange   Red   Yellow

We have improved the official Carbon Shinai rubber stopper.
The NEW official rubber stopper.
¥300 (domestic Japanese price)

WARNING!! Never use anything other than our official rubber stopper on your Carbon Shinai !!

When using your Carbon Shinai.....

1. To prevent injury, please use our official rubber stopper. Do not use stoppers made for conventional bamboo shinai on your Carbon Shinai, as there is a risk of injury to your opponent if the tip breaks through and enters their men grill.
2. When choosing a sakigawa (leather tip), make sure that it is more than 5cm in length and completely covers our rubber stopper. If the sakigawa is shorter than 5cm, there is a risk of injury to your opponent if a slat slips out and enters their men grill.
3. Do not shave the plastic surface of your Carbon Shinai. If you shave the surface, the black carbon fiber will be exposed, causing damage that may result in injury to your opponent.
4. Always check the condition of the surface of your Carbon Shinai before and during use. As soon as you notice any cracks, or peeling of the surface, or if black carbon fiber is exposed on any part of the outside, inside or edges of the Shinai, or you notice any other damage, stop using the shinai immediately. There is a danger of injury to your opponent if your Carbon Shinai is split or broken.
5. When tying the nakayui (leather binding), either tie a knot in the tsuru-ito (cord), or tie one end of the nakayui to the tsuru-ito, or by another means ensuring that is does not move up and down during use. If there is any damage whatsoever to the sakigawa, tsukagawa (hilt), rubber stopper, tsuru-ito and so on, replace them immediately.
6. If the tip of the Carbon Shinai is damaged, or a slat is protuding out of the sakigawa, there is a danger that it could enter your opponent's men grill and injure them.

Kendogu Revolution

Mu-Jun Men
武楯面

WARNING!!

1. Under no circumstances should organic solvents (such as thinner, alcohol, benzene, toluene, acetone, gasoline, kerosene, etc.), acidic or alkali chemicals, domestic cleansers, car cleansers, or anti-mist sprays, be used to clean the shield. These substances will cause the shield to deteriorate, leading to clouding, cracking or breaking, thereby resulting in danger of injury to the face.
2. Should the shield develop deep scratches or cracks on either the outer or inner surface, discontinue use of the shield immediately, and replace it with an undamaged shield. If the shield is used in such a condition, there is a danger of it breaking, causing injury to the face.
3. It should be fully understood that, as with the traditional Japanese Kendo-Men (mask), there is still the danger of injury to the face through fragments of broken bamboo or Carbon Shinai pieces penetrating through areas not covered by the shield.

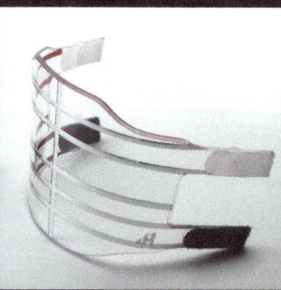
SG-Type

- SCIENCE TO SEEK SAFETY -
HASEGAWA
HASEGAWA CORPORATION

WEB : http://kendo.hasegawakagaku.co.jp/
Email : contact@hasegawakagaku.co.jp

Carbon Shinai — Points to be checked

DANGER!! **ATTENTION!!**

Before these happen.....

Although the Carbon Shinai is much more durable than a conventional bamboo one, it will inevitably become damaged since it is a sword that is used to repeatedly strike and thrust your opponent. Therefore, inspect the condition of the surface, sides or reverse of the Carbon Shinai's slats before, during and after use, and stop using it immediately should damage like in the following pictures be observed. (These pictures are just a few examples of many.)

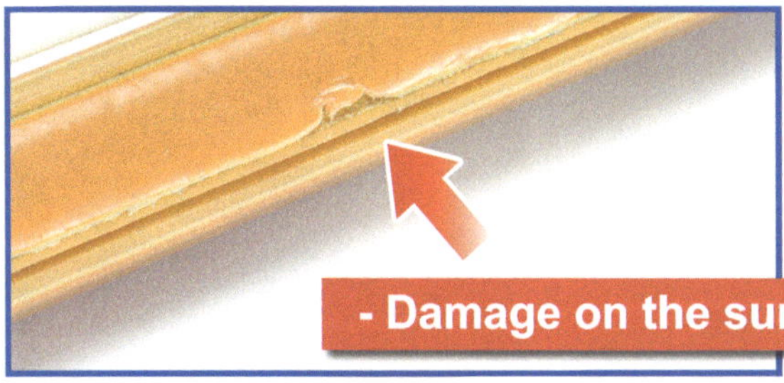

- Damage on the surface
- An unglued surface sheet 
- Exposure of the Carbon fiber 
- Longitudinal crack on the surface 
- Damage and ungluing of the surface 
- Crack on the reverse

There is the case where the reverse gets cracked even without any damage on the surface. Inspect the inside of the Shinai by pushing the pieces with the fingers and unbinding the Naka-yui.

HASEGAWA-KOTE

- Detachable and washable "Tenouchi" is easy to wash and dry.
- "Tenouchi" is replaceable when torn. No need to repair.

Tenouchi (Inner) *Kote (Main part)*

- SCIENCE TO SEEK SAFETY -
HASEGAWA

HASEGAWA CORPORATION
http://kendo.hasegawakagaku.co.jp/

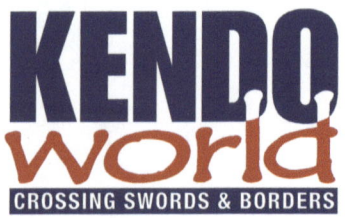

PUBLICATIONS

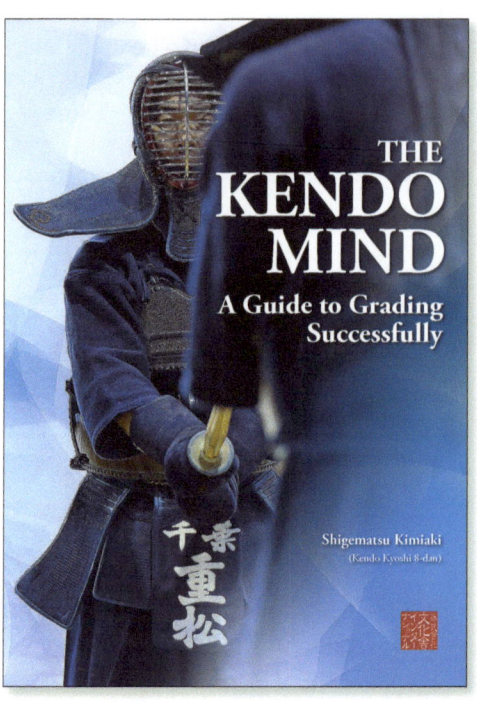

Naginata
Naginata, History and Practice

Of the handful of books on Naginata that do exist, most are prewar Japanese textbooks which are for the most part irrelevant to the popular form of Naginata developed in the post-war period. Postwar Naginata books are scant, and usually only cover the same basic techniques. Very little information is offered in regards to the cultural, historical, and mental aspects of Naginata. It requires a concerted effort to find such information in Japanese books, and to date, apart from a few journal articles, there has been virtually no work done in these areas in English or any other language. Until now, Naginata practitioners around the world have been left almost completely in the dark with regard to how the modern art that we practise today actually evolved and took its current form, in a process that spanned over one thousand years. This book fills the gap.

The Kendo Mind:
A Guide to Grading Successfully

Those who study kendo regard examinations and matches as vehicles for cultivating self-discipline and skill. Preparing to take a grading is especially motivating compared to regular training. It is, however, also a tremendous disappointment when you fail. There are those who manage to pass each examination without ever failing, and others who reach an impasse. So, what is the difference between these two groups? If you can figure it out, even just a little, you are one step closer to finding success. There are many things needed to pass an examination, not least of which is impressing the judges with resonating strikes. There is no way to achieve your goal without knowing how to accomplish this. The content of this book is based on lessons I learned from my sensei, my personal experiences in the dojo, and what I read in books and instruction manuals along the way. I hope that you will find the information in this small volume useful reference material as you navigate the path of kendo.

More info → www.kendo-world.com

KENDO WORLD Volume 8.2 June 2016 Contents

Editorial The Living National Treasures of Kendo — 2

The 14th All Japan Invitational 8-dan Kendo Tournament — 6

UTS Kendo Seminar
An Interview with Takanabe Susumu and Wakō Daisuke — 10

Takano Sasaburō's *Kendō: Chapter 2* — 15

Kendo for Adults — 22

Uncle Kotay's Kendo Korner
Part 2: The pleats in the hakama — 29

Kendo From Basics — 30

Reidan-jichi Part 21 **Hiki-waza** — 34

sWords of Wisdom
"Geisha no kokoro sutetsubeshi" — 36

The Life of Hayashizaki Jinsuke Minamoto no Shigenobu — 38

BOOK MARK
Kendo: Culture of the Sword — 44

Rene van Amersfoort: Jodo 8-dan — 46

Bujutsu Jargon Part 9 — 48

A Guide to Japanese Armour — 50

The Shugyō Mind: Part 2 — 54

The Rokudan Road — 56

Kendo Teachings — 60

Hagakure and the Ideal of Preparedness — 64

K8-dan Roberto Kishikawa-sensei's Kendo Seminar in São Carlos, Brazil — 66

**Musō Jikiden Eishin-ryū Riai
The Meaning of the Kata: Part 4** — 72

Dojo File
Nenriki Dojo: 50 Years — 80

Average Rank for a Dojo — 82

The Dual Path of Sword and Brush — 87

Shinai Sagas
The Secret of My School — 94

Inishie wo Kangaeru — 98

Kendo World Staff
- Bunkasha International President & Editor-in-Chief— Alex Bennett PhD
- Bunkasha International Vice President & Assistant Editor—Michael Ishimatsu-Prime MA
- Bunkasha International Vice President & Graphic Design—Shishikura 'Kan' Masashi
- Bunkasha International Vice President—Hamish Robison
- Bunkasha International Vice President—Michael Komoto MA
- Bunkasha International General Manager—Baptiste Tavernier MA
- Senior Consultants—Yonemoto Masayuki, Shima Masahiko

KW Staff Writers / Translators / Photographers / Graphic Designer / Sub-editors
- Axel Pilgrim PhD
- Blake Bennett PhD
- Bruce Flanagan MA
- Bryan Peterson
- Charlie Kondek
- Gabriel Weitzner
- Honda Sōtarō PhD
- Imafuji Masahiro MBA
- Jeff Broderick
- Kate Sylvester PhD
- Okuura Ayako
- Sergio Boffa PhD
- Stephen Nagy PhD
- Steven Harwood MA
- Takubo Seiya
- Taylor Winter
- Tony Cundy
- Trevor Jones
- Tyler Rothmar
- Yamaguchi Remi
- Vivian Yung
- Yulin Zhuang

KW would like to thank the following people and organisations for their valuable cooperation:
- All Japan Kendo Federation
- Hasegawa Teiichi - President, Hasegawa Corporation
- *Kendo Jidai* Magazine
- *Kendo Nihon* Magazine
- Nippon Budokan Foundation
- Nine Circles
- Shogun Kendogu
- TOZANDO

Guest Writers
- Carolina Akemi Martins Morita (São Carlos, Brazil)
- Clement Guo (UTS Kendo Club, Sydney)
- Gil Vicente Nagai Lourenção (São Carlos, Brazil)
- Hatano Toshio (Kendo Kyōshi 8-dan)
- Hirakawa Nobuo (Kendo Kyōshi 8-dan)
- Iwadate Saburō (Kendo Hanshi 8-dan)
- Jack James (Jūshinden)
- Jo Anseeuw (Association for the Research and Preservation of Japanese Helmets and Armour)
- Kenji Nakahara Rocha (São Carlos, Brazil)
- Kim Taylor (Iaido 7-dan, sdksupplies.com)
- Kurt Schmucker (U.S. Naginata Federation, President)
- Ōya Minoru (Prof. International Budo University; Kendo Kyōshi 7-dan)
- Sue Lytollis (New Zealand Women's Coach, Kendo 6-dan)
- Victor Harris (Nenriki Dojo)
- Yashiro Yamamoto (São Carlos, Brazil)

COPYRIGHT 2016 Bunkasha International Corporation. No part of this publication may be reproduced in any form whatsoever without written permission from the publisher, except by writers who are permitted to quote brief passages for the purpose of review or reference. Kindly contact Bunkasha International Corporation at info@kendo-world.com.

Editorial Conventions Used in KW Inevitably in a magazine of this nature, many non-English words appear in the text. All Japanese words are italicised and include macrons (ū, ō) etc., apart from common place names and nouns, and words in some captions and headings. As a general exception, KW treats all the martial arts (budo), such as kendo, iaido, jodo, ranks, and so on as Anglicised words without using macrons. Japanese names are written in accordance to the traditional Japanese manner of family name followed by given name. Traditional *ryūha* are written with capitals and therefore are not italicised. 'Kata' with a capital 'K' refers to the set of Nippon Kendo Kata, and *kata* refers to set forms in general. The masculine personal pronoun is used throughout the text in some articles in the interest of readability, and is in no way meant to slight the significant contributions made by female kendoka.

Editorial
The Living National Treasures of Kendo
By Alex Bennett

It took four years to make but it's here now, at last. The problem is, it's so good, and so goddam expensive, I don't want to use it. I couldn't bear the thought of somebody's *shinai* leaving a mark on any patch of my made-to-perfection set of super *bōgu*. How much? Let me just say it would make your eyes water. It did mine, and my wife is never ever to know. Can I afford it? Not really to be perfectly honest, even on my comparatively generous university salary and with no "ankle-biters" to feed or care for. Still, when I was told by an old *bōgu* dealer friend, Mr. Tokusanai, at my sensei's BBQ some years back that the *futon* used in the finest-of-fine craftsman-fashioned *bōgu* is as rare as hen's teeth, but that he can get his hands on panels stitched by the last Mohican, my *sake*-lubricated jolly brain just had to get me some. I ordered (I think) a full set of *bōgu* with only the finest trimmings. He measured me on the spot… It wasn't hard to justify it to myself; I thought that it would be a lifetime set only for VERY special occasions like 8-dan examination(s), and if I don't get it now, the craft of traditional *bōgu* making by the last generation of genuine artisans would pass me by. It was now or never.

I had plenty of time to put away a bit of money each month, but of course I didn't. When I saw an incoming call from Tokusanai-san appear on my iPhone screen recently, I knew I was in for a financial lashing. But, I also knew it would be worth it. I travelled from Kyoto to Chiba last week to pick it up. Seeing the gorgeous creation placed before me on the table was nothing short of magical. It was everything I dreamed it would be, only more beautiful. The immaculate stitching in the thin but impenetrable and highly malleable *futon*, the perfection and detail in the assembly, the seamlessness of the fit, the splendid leather appurtenances made of only premium quality materials, the smoky fresh odour of untainted *bōgu*… It is a work of art. It even has its own aura, and an attitude that says, "Are you really worthy of me, Bennett?"

Okay, I know I've been doing kendo for too long when I start talking about a new set of equipment as if it were the second coming of Christ. I have a serious kendo habit, and have plenty of *bōgu* sets to suit many occasions. They are all good quality; most are hand-stitched and order made. Many *bōgu* retailers will have you believe that their wares are "Made in Japan", so

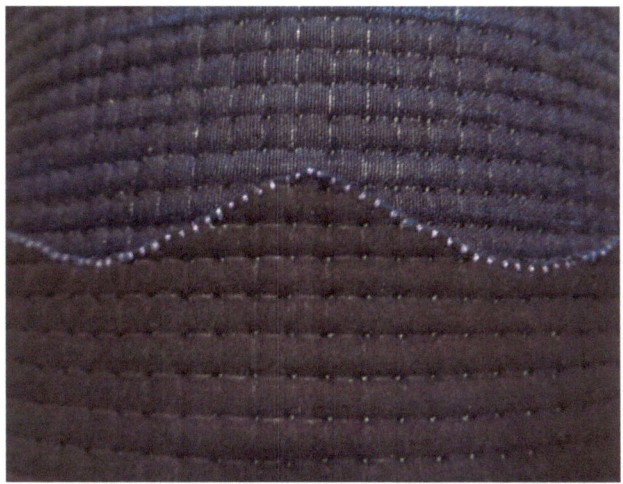

there is no need to concern yourself with the quality. This may or may not be the case, depending on the retailer, but it is hardly disputed anymore that most *bōgu* purchased in or through Japan is actually made offshore. It may be assembled in Japan, but nine times out of ten the pieces are stitched together in factories outside the country. That is not to say that *futon* produced in China, Korea, Indonesia, the Philippines, Japanese prisons, or wherever, is necessarily bad. If you want a reasonably priced set of gear which looks smart and will last you more than a few years of rigorous training, then $1000 will set you right in this day and age. You could pay more, but I wouldn't pay less. The price for *bōgu* has truly gone through the floor. Sadly, the kendo population is shrinking in Japan and the little Ma and Pa neighbourhood kendo shops can't compete with the big boys and their offshore resources. Many are shutting up shop. Welcome to globalisation.

Thus, the issue of price wars in the *bōgu* world is a proverbial double-edged sword. Producing components offshore is cheap, and consumers are happy to get their hands on inexpensive, disposable equipment. The downside is that the traditional art of *bōgu* making in Japan is rapidly dying out. A craftsman cannot match the speed and pricing of the low-cost stuff, which doesn't look that different to the undiscerning eye. The return for sitting cross-legged on a *tatami* mat from morning to night, hunched over squinting while pushing needles through thick padding and trying to keep each stitch in a perfect line, is far from satisfactory. It's not an easy life, and not surprisingly few want to take up an apprenticeship anymore. When the last of the old artisans passes away, there will be nobody to inherit their skills and knowhow to continue the craft for the kendoka of tomorrow.

Alas, the old artisans are almost all gone. That's why it took four years for my *bōgu* to be completed. There is nobody left in Japan now who can make an entire set. The *kote*, *men*, *dō* and *tare* were all painstakingly made by different artisans, with Tokusanai-san coordinating the group effort like a true Kantoku. Apparently, the craftsman who assembled the *men* made a small mistake. A strip of leather that he stitched onto the *futon* was "not the right shape". I had absolutely no idea what he was talking about when I was shown it, but Tokusanai-san ordered him to make another one from scratch, using the very last panel of the precious *futon*. "Only perfection will suffice," he told me, but to my great joy, I was given the castoff as well. In spite of its "defect", it's worth thousands.

Editorial

It is clearly evident, even to a kendo novice (I ended up showing my wife, but didn't tell her the [real] cost) how superior the work of an experienced artisan is compared to a decent mass-produced item. The difference in quality is incontestable. It occurred to me that a significant part of kendo is dying in Japan. I have heard about the dwindling *bōgu* craftsmen, as we all have at some stage, but it really is a critical issue. One of the problems is that the artisans themselves are extremely protective of their techniques, and don't want to make them common knowledge. They would traditionally pass on their sublime skills to apprentices, but there are none. With each craftsman that disappears, so too does a wealth of experience and secret techniques.

What can be done, then, to preserve this dying art? Practically speaking, I fear not much. My set will surely be my last even though I desperately want to support the craftsmen, and most people are not inclined to spend as much as a medium-sized car on kendo equipment. Nevertheless, I believe that more needs to be done by the governors of kendo to acknowledge the craft as an indispensable aspect of kendo's tradition. Like global warming, the damage has really already been done, but it is not too late to bring the art into the limelight to be appreciated not only by kendo aficionados, but all people who appreciate fine craft. The workmanship is on par with any of the famous and highly lauded artists in Japan, it's just that nobody knows about them.

Japan has an interesting system called "Living National Treasure" for individuals or groups certified as "Preservers of Important Intangible Cultural Properties". This prestigious status is designated by the Minister of Education, Culture, Sports, Science and Technology and is based on the "Law for the Protection of Cultural Properties". Intangible cultural properties refer to certain artistic skills, and those who are perceived as having attained mastery in those skills are selected as "preservers" by the government for the purpose of ensuring their continuation. A look at the list of Living National Treasures in crafts (the other category being performing arts) reveals potters, lacquer ware producers, paper makers, metal workers, wood workers, doll makers and so on, but no *bōgu* makers, or *shinai* craftsmen for that matter.

It seems to me that there is something very wrong with this situation, and lamentably I suspect that true kendo artisans will only be recognised by the powers that be when there are none left. With that in mind, *Kendo World* is in the process of lobbying the All Japan Kendo Federation to see if something can be done to acknowledge the few remaining masters of our beloved kendo—not the hitters this time, but the stitchers, carvers, lacquerers, dyers, and the *shinai* "smiths". It would be wonderful if they too could be designated as "Living National Treasures", and rewarded for their contribution to kendo culture.

Meanwhile, I must make an executive decision: am I worthy enough to try that *men* on for the first time in *keiko* today? What the hey! It was made to be used, so in the bag it goes! (Post[*keiko*]script: OMG! How can I ever go back?)

重要無形文化財保持者
Jūyō Mukei Bunkazai Hojisha

Preserver of Important Intangible Cultural Properties

These people are recognised by the Japanese government as "...individuals or groups who embody to an outstanding degree the relevant skills or crafts, in order to promote the transmission of Japan's traditional skills and crafts."

人間国宝 (芸能,)
Ningen Kokuhō (Geinō)

National Living Treasure (Performing Arts)

Current holders of this title can be found in Noh, Bunraku, Kabuki, Kumi Odori, music, dance and drama.

人間国宝 (工芸技術)
Ningen Kokuhō (Kōgei Gijutsu)

National Living Treasure (Crafts)

Holders of this title are skilled in traditional Japanese crafts that are divided into the categories of dollmaking, lacquerware, metalworking, papermaking, pottery, textiles, woodworking, and other.

PUBLICATIONS

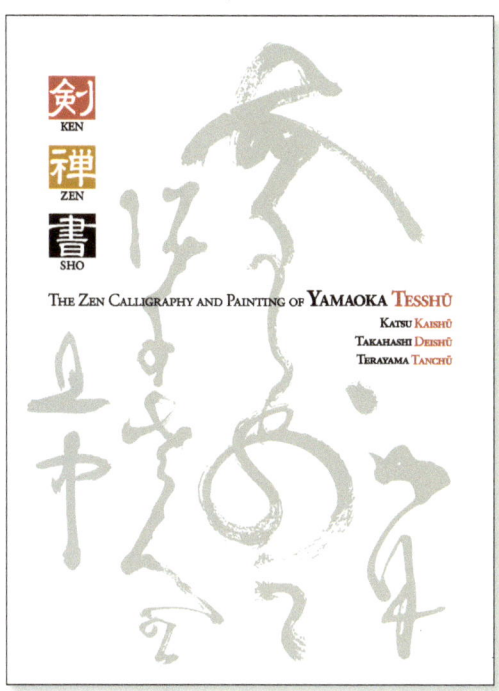

Ken Zen Sho
The Zen Calligraphy and Painting of Yamaoka Tesshu

Yamaoka Tesshu (1836-1888) was a Japanese master of the sword, Zen and calligraphy. This full-colour book on the Zen art of Yamaoka Tesshu features reproductions of extremely valuable calligraphy pieces, and also a number of essays about the relationship between swordsmanship, the study of Zen, and calligraphy. Each one of the works presented is translated into English, and its significance explained in detailed captions. Some fantastic specimens of Zen calligraphy by Tesshu's famous contemporaries Katsu Kaishu and Takahashi Deishu (Tesshu's brother-in-law), and modern master Terayama Tanchu are also featured.

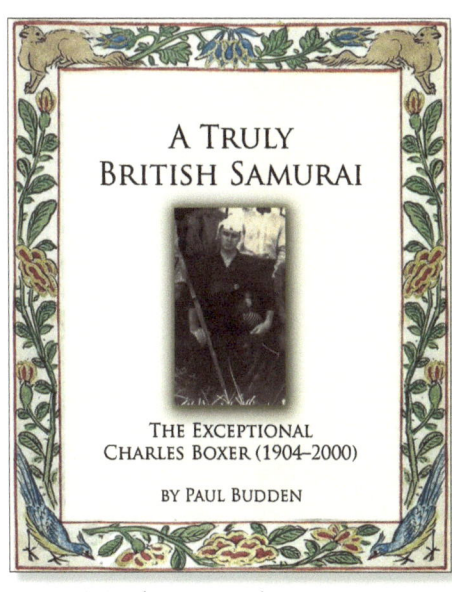

A Truly British Samurai
The Exceptional Charles Boxer

Budo Perspectives

Kendo:
Approaches for all Levels

More info → www.kendo-world.com

Furukawa Kazuo (Hokkaido) scores a *men* against Shimizu Shinji (Kumamoto) in the first round.

Shimizu Shinji (Kumamoto) attempts a *men* against Furukawa Kazuo (Hokkaido) but is unsuccessful.

The 14th All Japan Invitational 8-dan Kendo Tournament

Nakamura Sports Center, Nagoya—Sunday 17th April, 2016

Text: Michael Ishimatsu-Prime/Photos: Alex Bennett

The fourteenth edition of the 8-dan holders tournament was held again at Nakamura Sports Center in Nagoya. As predicted, it turned out to be a great tournament with some magnificent performances by highly skilled and experienced sensei. Of note were K8-dan Hirano Seiji (Tokushima) who ruthlessly dispatched former champion Ishida Toshiya (Tokyo) in the first round; Kanagawa's diminutive K8-dan Kasamura Kōji; K8-dan Koyama Masahiro (Shizuoka), who dismantled two-time champion K8-dan Funatsu Shinji (Osaka); and of course, six-time All Japan Champion, K8-dan Miyazaki Masahiro (Kanagawa), who was crowned champion in his second appearance in the championships Videos of all the matches from the quarter-finals onwards can be seen on our YouTube channel, but here are some of the choice photographs that we took on the day.

Hirano Seiji (Tokushima) lands a *tsuki* against Ishida Toshiya (Tokyo) in the first round.

After Ishida Toshiya levels the match against Hirano Seiji with a *men* strike, Hirano scores *men-kaeshi-dō* to win this enthralling first round encounter.

Koyama Masahiro (Shizuoka) scores his second *men* against Funatsu Shinji (Osaka).

K8-dan Miyazaki Masahiro after defeating H8-dan Ishizuka Yoshifumi in the first round.

Matsumoto Masashi (Kagawa) defeats Kasamura Kōji (Kanagawa) with a *kote* in *enchō*.

In the semi-final, Miyazaki Masahiro (right) attempts to strike the *dō* of Koyama Masahiro (Shizuoka).

In the final, Miyazaki Masahiro (left) scores his second *men* strike against Matsumoto Masashi to win the tournament in style.

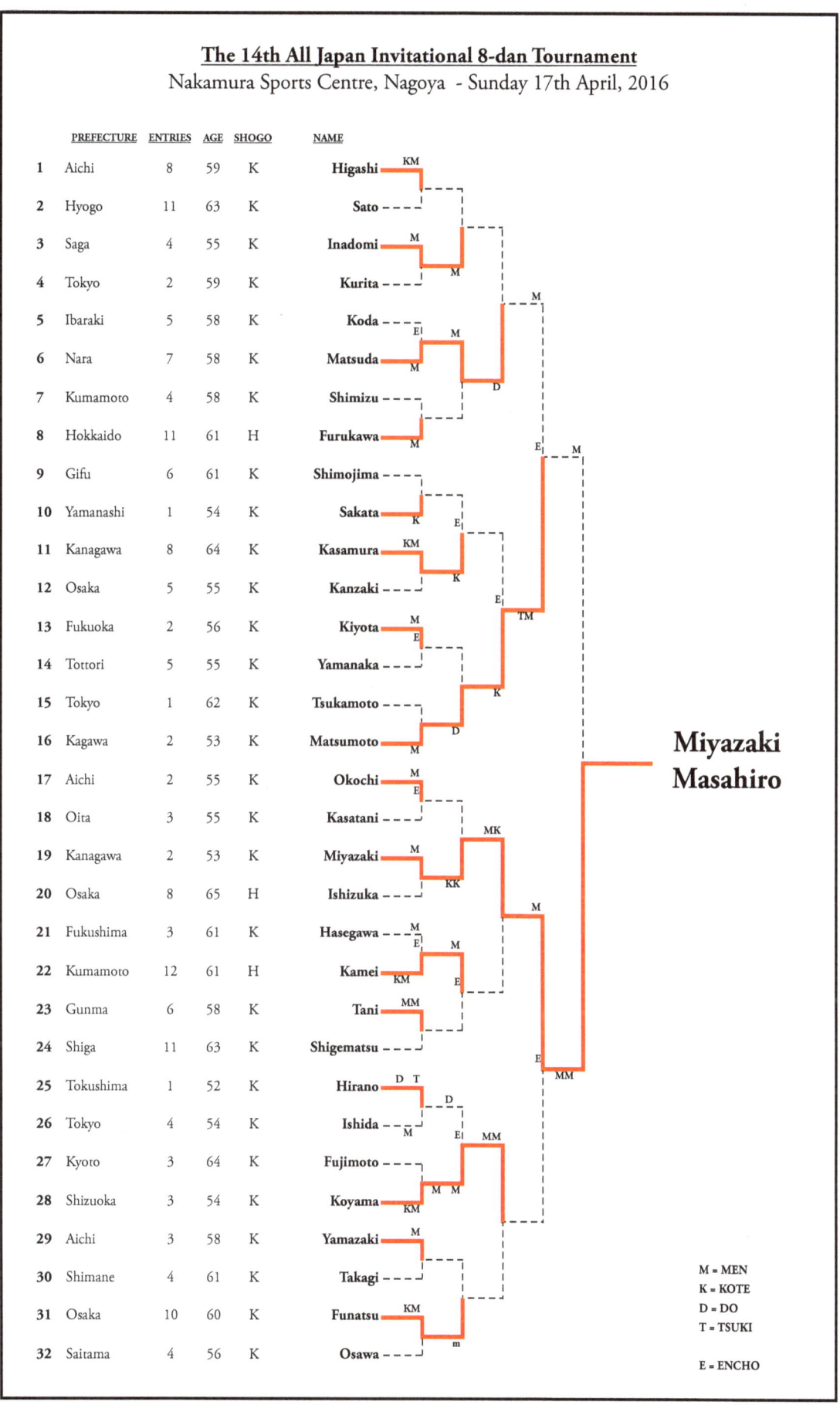

UTS KENDO SEMINAR

An Interview with
TAKANABE Susumu and WAKŌ Daisuke

By Clement Guo
Photos by Taek Yang and John Ou

On December 3 & 4, 2015, UTS Kendo Club in Sydney, Australia, hosted its inaugural seminar, and invited two internationally renowned sensei, R7-dan Takanabe Susumu and R7-dan Wakō Daisuke, from Japan to share their experiences and teach kendo.

Both sensei are highly regarded in kendo, having represented Japan at the World Kendo Championships (WKC). Takanabe-sensei represented Japan on four occasions, winning the Men's Individual Championships at the 2012 WKC in Italy. He also won the All Japan Kendo Championships (AJKC) two years in a row in 2010 and 2011. Wakō-sensei also represented Japan at the 2009 WKC in Brazil and made it to the quarterfinals in the individual competition. Prior to this, he was the runner-up at the AJKC in 2008.

Over 85 participants from various countries gathered at the UTS dojo for the seminar that focused on the basics of *suburi*, *waza* training, and provided a rare opportunity to do *ji-geiko* with the sensei. During their short visit, *Kendo World* interviewed both Takanabe-sensei and Wakō-sensei to learn about their kendo background and how they prepare for a competition.

Kendo World: *Why do you do kendo and what does it mean to you?*

Takanabe-sensei: Kendo is a big part of my life. I started doing it in my childhood and have continued all through my life. Even now as a police officer in Kanagawa prefecture, I do kendo as part of my job. As such, I always think about kendo, and it is something I cannot live without.

Wakō-sensei: I have also been doing kendo since I

was a young lad, and it is something I enjoy. In fact, my passion for kendo was the reason why I joined the police in Hokkaido. I can do kendo as a part of my job.

Kendo World: *How do you prepare for a big competition such as the AJKF or WKC?*

Takanabe-sensei: My preparation and training routine does not change. The usual daily training at the police is very rigorous, and there is no special practice ahead of a competition. The training environment, however, does change a bit. For example, I do get to practice with the other Japanese representatives leading up to a WKC when normally we would never train together.

Although my training routine does not change much, what becomes important in the lead up to any competition is maintaining concentration in my daily *keiko*. I reduce the number of cuts or strikes to focus on refinement. The menu and content remains pretty much the same—I don't add anything new at the last minute.

Takanabe Susumu

Wakō-sensei: I approach every competition the same way, regardless of how big or small it is. My training methods and objectives are constant, and centres on always trying to overcome my weaknesses. The nature of a competition does not make any difference to me. I place a very high standard on myself in training and this does not change ahead of any tournament.

Kendo World: *Aside from keiko, how else do you physically or mentally prepare for competitions? Do you follow a specific diet or exercise routine?*

[*Before giving a specific answer, both Takanabe-sensei and Wakō-sensei discussed that they train in kendo for most of the day, five days a week. When they are not training, they are teaching kendo to others. The opportunities to do kendo are plentiful and they do not often find themselves with spare time to focus on supplementary activities.*]

Takanabe-sensei: In addition to kendo practice, and not simply just as preparation for a competition, I work on leg and core body exercises. This includes running, sit ups, and back muscle exercises. With regards to my diet, I gradually eat more carbohydrates like rice or

Wakō Daisuke

pasta, which gives me the necessary energy.

Wakō-sensei: I prefer doing *suburi* as well as lower body exercises (e.g. runs, sprints). I think this provides greater benefits in kendo than upper body workouts and weight training. For my mental preparation, I reflect on my daily *keiko*, and try to be confident in the knowledge that my routine has prepared me well. As for diet, I simply try not to eat and drink too much!

Kendo World: *Do you get nervous during a competition? If so, how do you maintain your composure and keep calm in order to perform well?*

Takanabe-sensei: I do get nervous during a competition, but I don't think of it as a bad thing. In fact, I find that I function best when I am nervous, but being able to control your nerves and not get too worked up is important. I try to imagine my best performance on the day, and avoid thinking too much about the opponent.

Wakō-sensei: I also get nervous; everyone is afraid of losing. But holding onto this thought is not good. I think of what I did in training and remind myself that I am in the best shape. Then I just concentrate on the opponent in front of me, and forget about the rest!

Kendo World: *Do you approach individual and team competitions differently?*

Takanabe-sensei: Basic training and mental preparation is the same. However, in a team competition, the outcome of the match before your own can impact your strategy. Sometimes, you have to win in five minutes, but other times it is OK to draw. Your usual training regime should prepare you for every situation.

Wakō-sensei: For me, there is no difference in preparation. My physical and mental training is always the same.

Kendo World: *What has been the most nerve-wracking tournament for you?*

Takanabe-sensei and Wakō-sensei: The WKC!

Kendo World: *From your experience, what are some of the big mistakes people make during a match?*

Takanabe-sensei: From my experience, I find that if I think too much about the opponent, I am unable to perform my best in the match.

Wakō-sensei: I agree. At some level, everyone is afraid of getting hit or losing, but it's important not to dwell on these negative thoughts; otherwise you cannot perform at your highest level.

Kendo World: *Does participating in a competition as a shinpan help towards one's understanding and effectiveness in shiai? Conversely, is it important to be an active kendoka to be a good shinpan?*

Takanabe-sensei: I think being a *shinpan* is good for one's kendo development. When I was a competitor, I was rarely able to serve as a *shinpan*. As I move more into a coaching role, I am seeing the benefits of being a *shinpan* in understanding competition strategy, and what is correct or incorrect kendo.

Wakō-sensei: Yes, it is important to participate as a *shinpan*. The role of *shinpan* carries the responsibility of knowing all of the various *waza*, and being able to award an *ippon*. Therefore, you should always try your best to execute various *waza* in your training, not just the ones you are good at. This will not only develop your kendo, but also contribute towards your capability as a *shinpan*.

Kendo World: *As you move into a coaching role, what important lessons will you pass on to your students?*

Takanabe-sensei: An important thing I would like to pass on to students is to always learn with an open mind. Often a teacher's advice may seem challenging or hard to grasp at first, but don't be afraid to give it a go!

Wakō-sensei: As discussed in the seminar, I think it is important to build a strong foundation of correct kendo. This starts with doing *suburi*, and correctly practising footwork and movements, which then enables you to perform various *waza* and learn the right timing. This in turn culminates in *ippon* at competitions.

Kendo World: *What advice do you have for new beginners competing for the first time?*

Takanabe-sensei: It is important to have fun and enjoy it. Winning and losing is not important.

Wakō-sensei: I agree. As a kendo teacher for young kids back in Japan, I care about having fun doing kendo. This means praising them when they do well, and working positively to improve their kendo further. Winning and losing is not as important in their first outing in the competitive arena.

Kendo World: *Takanabe-sensei and Wakō-sensei, thank you very much.*

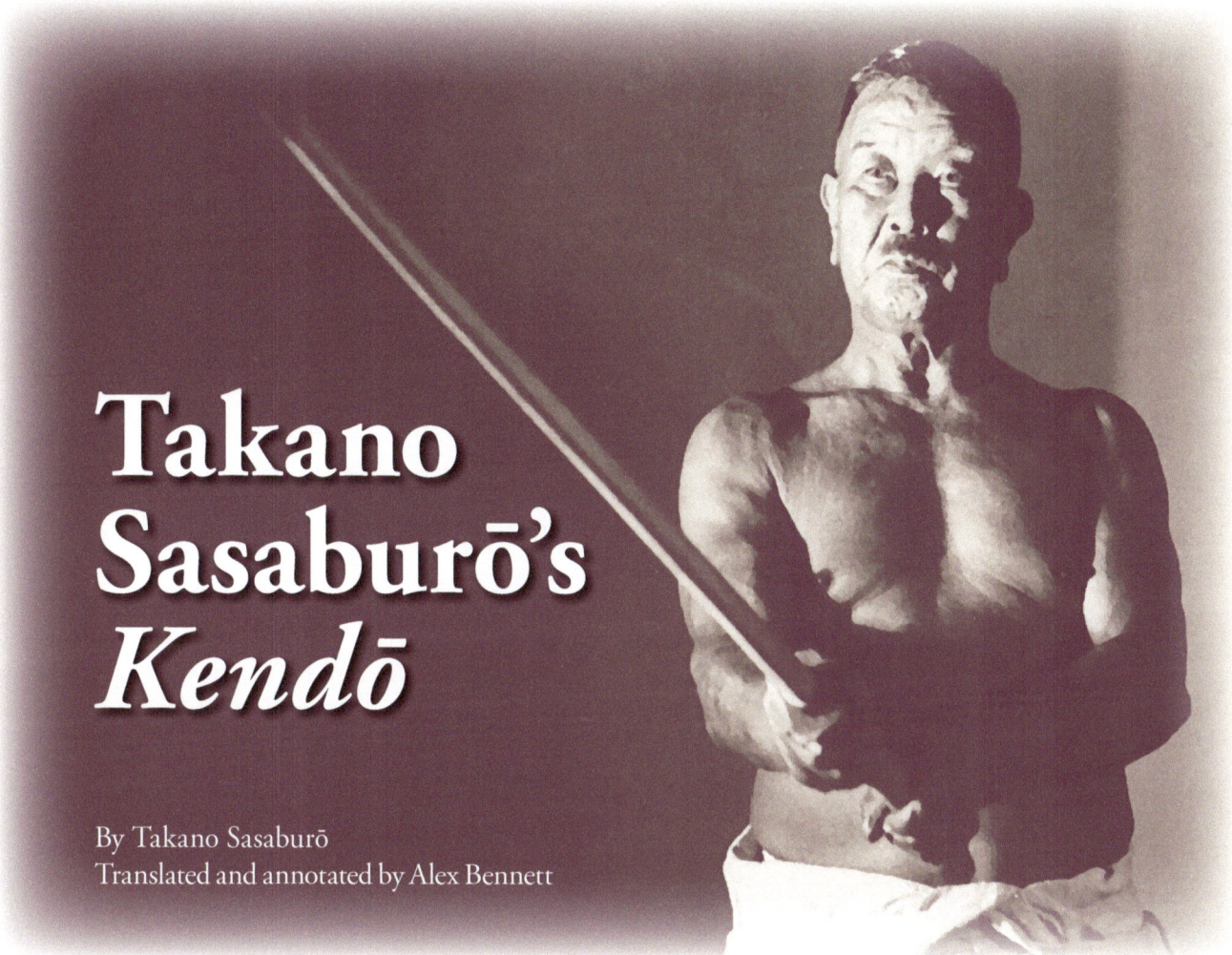

Takano Sasaburō's *Kendō*

By Takano Sasaburō
Translated and annotated by Alex Bennett

Takano Sasaburō (1862–1950) is considered to be one of the most influential pioneers of modern kendo. He was instrumental in developing the *dan* grading system for kendo, and was also a key member in the committee that created the Kendo Kata in 1912. His book, simply titled *Kendō*, was a *tour de force* in the creation of a uniform style for modern kendo, and is still considered a classic by kendoka today. In this series of articles, I will translate Takano's book, and annotate the text to contextualise its ground-breaking content. The following is Chapter 2 of *Kendō*.

Chapter 2: Kendo in Schools

Section 1—The Objective of Kendo in Education

As I have already established in the previous chapter, the true aim of kendo is to anneal the body and mind. This objective is no different in schools where kendo is taught as a part of the physical education curriculum. A summary of PE teaching content can be found in Article 13 of the "National Middle School Curriculum". Nagai Michiaki covers the gist of it clearly in his book, *Gakkō taisō yogi* (The essentials of school PE):

The purpose for teaching PE is to facilitate the overall balanced physical development and full augmentation of bodily functions to maintain health and wellbeing. Course content is designed to encourage agility and dexterity in movement, and a vigorous and resilient mind. It also seeks to teach students the importance of abiding by rules and respecting collective protocols.

Kendo can also realise these objectives if taught judiciously, and there were attempts made in the past to adapt kendo into a viable alternative to calisthenics—an initiative which was by no means without merit. Nevertheless, an important characteristic of kendo is its rigor. This is what sets kendo apart from various methods of developmental and corrective exercises. Therefore, if the stated objectives for physical education in schools is to be accomplished through the medium of kendo, then this would necessitate a compromise of its underlying characteristics. In any case, callisthenics and drills are already employed in the school setting for these purposes, so there is really no need to try and achieve the same goals through kendo. If kendo is to be utilised in some capacity to fulfil PE's stipulated objectives, nurturing agility and dexterity in movement, and a vigorous and resilient mind would be more than reasonable. As stated in the MoE's "Principal Points for Teaching Physical Education in Schools":

> Although the focus of kendo and judo education is to forge the body and mind, more weight should be given to mental training. Technical instruction simply for the purpose of winning matches should be discouraged.

Clearly kendo is also beneficial for physical growth, full development of bodily functions, and overall health and wellbeing. Thus, whilst being fully aware that kendo perfectly valid as a PE exercise, efforts should be made to accentuate its unique characteristics and the benefits that can be gained thereof. With this in mind, attention is best directed to the clause stating that "more weight should be given to mental training."

It is easy to forgo the true aims of kendo to concentrate on developing techniques and flashy skills for the sake of winning competitions. Indeed, this is often the case. Such motivations impede spiritual training through kendo. This is particularly so with children who are wont to forget the inherent mind-set underlying kendo in lieu of ostentatious designs and a drive to seek sophisticated techniques well before they are ready. Children also have a tendency to be excessively competitive, and need to be reprimanded on occasion to keep them on the right track.

The time designated for the study of kendo in schools is extremely limited. Within curriculum time constraints, the teacher is required to impart a considerable body of instructional content. To facilitate adequate technical progress is difficult even with extracurricular lessons. Along with technical improvement, efforts must be made to give students a thorough drilling in the basics (*kihon*), make sure that they develop correct posture, and build a strong body and mind through demanding training. The purpose of teaching kendo in schools is not to nurture expert kendoka *per se*, but to entice students to become interested in the Way of kendo. Ideally, they will then decide through their own volition to pursue the study of kendo at a higher level after graduating.

In the "Principal Points for Teaching Physical Education in Schools" it states,

> Exercise on a daily basis should never be neglected. To this end, it behoves schools to ensure that pupils are aware of the importance of physical activity so that it becomes routine in the home and after graduation from school.

In Japan, there are many options to choose from in schools when it comes to games and sports. However, opportunities outside of the school environment are few and far between. Some physical pursuits are difficult to participate in due to expense or the lack of appropriate facilities. Others require a minimum number of people to convene, so there are few sports that are readily accessible in the community. Kendo and judo, on the other hand, are not subjected to such obstacles, and are highly suited to the Japanese disposition. Kendo in particular has a time-honoured tradition, holds peoples' interest, is relatively safe to practise, can be participated in by young and old alike, and is appreciated by both practitioners and spectators. It is perfect as a communal exercise for self-improvement and as a form of recreation. Furthermore, as I mentioned in the previous chapter, kendo is effective for annealing the mind and body. If interest can be piqued in schools, with encouragement students will hopefully continue to a higher level after graduating. It behoves kendo practitioners to propagate kendo as much as possible in the community. It is our responsibility to ensure students continue.

Section 2—Teaching Content and Apportioning

Broadly speaking, there are two types of teaching content in kendo which can be further divided into four sub-categories. I will cover these in the next chapter.

1. Basic Training—Fundamental Movements (done solo, includes sequences)
   Kata
2. Partnered Practice Drills—Combined Training
   Sparring (*gokaku*)

In determining suitable tasks for each year group, objectives, type of content, and level of physical and mental maturity should be considered. Year-1 (12-years old) through to Year-3 (14-years old) in middle schools is a period of rapid growth. Children are not physically strong yet, and it is not advisable to subject them to excessively rigorous exercise. Some educators maintain the misguided opinion that even partnered training is inappropriate in this age group but they clearly know little about kendo. How harmful can two or three hours of kendo practice a week be? Even if there are minor risks involved, they can easily be allayed depending on how it is taught. If anything, children in this age group find practising with partners to be a thrilling experience and this enthusiasm should be exploited.

Moreover, in their innocence they do not hold back, and their flexible bodies enable lucid movement and freedom of the limbs. They are easy to teach, and so progress is speedy. Those aged 17 or 18, however, analyse things more and tend to show indecision. Their bodies are robust, but as they have more strength in their arms there is less autonomy of movement. They push through the discomfort, but will become disheartened as the physical demands prove too much to bear. Therefore, it is advisable to promote physical and technical development in children from early on, and teach both the fundamental movements as well as partnered drills. Just teaching the former without the opportunity to apply the techniques against an opponent will thwart the potential of kendo as an effective vehicle for mind-body training. On the other hand, having children engage in sparring when they are still technically inept, or not mature enough physically and mentally, will result in the formation of bad habits. Or, children may find training too challenging and start to dislike kendo as a result. In the initial stages, the teacher (or an experienced assistant) should join in as training partners, and allow children to spar on occasion, albeit under strict observation.

Six months of training in the fundamental movements should suffice to reach a degree of proficiency. The teacher may subsequently introduce combined training through which students learn how to apply the basic skills. They can then engage in free sparring with their peers (*gokaku-geiko*) under the watchful eye of the instructor. This will serve to deepen their interest in kendo.

Students in Year-4 and 5 will have matured physically, so partnered training is effective in helping them augment strength. Be heedful that their posture may deteriorate, and questionable technical habits will form if care is not taken. Revision of the fundamental movements should be conducted periodically to mitigate this, before and after partnered practice drills.

During combined training, the teacher and students put on their armour and work together, although beginners do not necessarily need to don the equipment. Teach students to seek appropriate striking opportunities, how to adapt to the circumstances, and how to apply the basics without falling into bad habits. Encourage them to engage with a cheerful disposition while demonstrating undaunted courage. Students must learn to be move with agility and build up their stamina. When sparring, students should be guided to make use of the techniques they have learned in attack and defence. Students need to engage in both training methods—solo exercises to review the basic movements, and partnered drills and free training to learn how to apply the techniques—so that optimum value can be extracted for nurturing physical and mental strength.

In addition to technical training, theoretical and spiritual instruction should not be forgotten. For example, the instructor must clearly explain the purpose of kendo and its objectives to new students.

As their ability improves, look for occasions to delve into the theory of kendo relaying biographical anecdotes of famous swordsmen. This will provide a source of fascination for students, hence expediting their progress and facilitating the aims of mind-body training.

Old stories of samurai heroics and swordsmanship are valuable teaching materials. Students can be made aware that what they are learning is not only relevant for classes in the dojo, but should be reflected on and embodied at all times. Teachers need to be thoughtful in their selection of materials to accomplish this goal. TABLE 1 is an indication of the amount of time spent on each training method for the different year groups. It is a basic overview for the allotment of class time for fundamental movements and partnered drills, but the point is that emphasising only one aspect should be avoided. When fundamental movements are the focus, time should also be allotted to spirited partnered

TABLE 1

Distribution of Kendo Teaching Content (Middle Schools)			
Timing	**1st Semester**	**2nd Semester**	**3rd Semester**
Year 1	· Required attitude and objectives · Explanation of sword parts (equipment) · Terminology · Handling the sword · Fundamental movements (up to basic striking)	· Fundamental movements (up to applied striking) · Partnered Practice Drills (first steps, *kirikaeshi*, *uchikomi* etc.)	· Fundamental movements (revision) · Partnered Practice Drills (combined, striking opportunities, bouts)
Year 2	· Fundamental movements (revision from previous year, combined movements) · Partnered Practice Drills (progress incrementally)	· Fundamental movements (same) · Partnered Practice Drills (same)	· Fundamental movements (same) · Partnered Practice Drills (same)
Year 3	· Fundamental movements (revision from previous year, *kata*) · Partnered Practice Drills (progress incrementally, gradually increasing sparring)	Same	Same
Year 4	Partnered Practice Drills (combined training and free sparring)	Same	Same
Year 5	Same as Year-4	Same	Same
Notes	One hour per week. The amount of time spent each week/semester on fundamental movements and partnered drills can be adjusted in accordance with progress.		

Year	Allocation of Time for Partnered Training and Fundamental Practice
1	
2	PARTNERED DRILLS
3	
4	FUNDAMENTAL MOVEMENTS
5	

drills. Conversely, when partnered drills are the focus, be sure to spend time on a thorough revision of the fundamental movements.

Section 3—Assessment

Assessing kendo classes is a complicated issue. It is not easy to implement one-size-fits-all criteria, but mental and physical progress still needs to be evaluated. ILLUSTRATION 1 shows approximate standards that can be applied in assessment. The percentage for each of the assessable factors (shown in parentheses) may be subject to change depending on the amount of time that can be spent on each one. For example, if one-third of total class time is used for basic training, the remaining two-thirds can be allocated to partnered drills. The weight put on each category can be modified to reflect the time spent on it.

Among the categories shown in the table there is little need to explain "posture" and "skill". Correct posture is developed in basic training, technical skills are polished, and fortitude nurtured to enable prolonged effort in training. Furthermore, stamina to withstand lengthy training sessions, and to maintain correct posture and execute techniques, is also crucial for wearing opponents down to prevail in bouts.

Skill does not necessarily equate to strength. Similarly, stamina is not always the premise of victory. "Strength and weakness" is not a simple issues as it also includes mental aspects. It is not necessary to dwell on such matters when teaching children. Manners and obedience to prescribed protocols of etiquette is all that is needed to ascertain the mental strength of a child. "Eagerness" is an indicator of the child's attitude and effort in kendo. Deep down inside, the child reflects and figures things out; and, this manifests externally as diligence. Those who show enthusiasm for kendo will rarely be absent and will not shirk off during class. Nevertheless, it is not adequate for a pupil to be diligent in one thing only. The child should be observant and speculative at all times, and always seek to work through matters of their own volition. Many children move together during basic practice, so discipline is a must. Of course, discipline is necessary during partnered training as well, but more so is having vim and vigour.

ILLUSTRATION 1

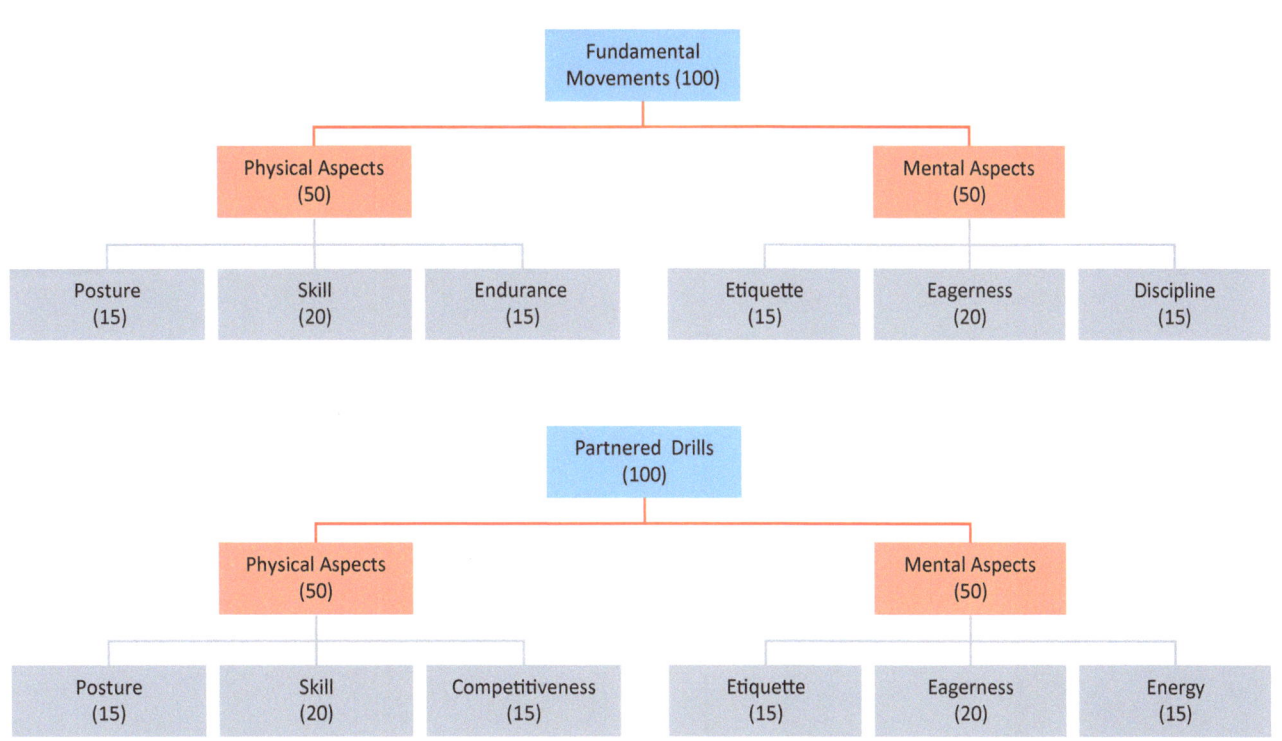

Section 4—Kendo Equipment

As outlined in the "School PE Curriculum Guidelines", "Equipment needs to be upgraded, and in the cases of both kendo and judo, a teaching methodology should be formulated to ensure that care is taken at all times to maintain hygiene."

Typical *bōgu* used in kendo nowadays is the result of many years of development, and is very nearly as good as it will ever get. It is dangerous to use *bōgu* that is poor in quality or is damaged in any way. Of the problems involving kendo equipment, the matter of hygiene is most pressing, and strikes to the *men* can be painful. *Men* that are constructed of particularly thin padding, or that are worn through will not prevent pain for the wearer when struck, and could even result in burst eardrums. Damage to the eardrums can be prevented by bolstering the ear with cotton before putting the *men* on. The inside of the *men* will become soiled with sweat and spit and must be kept clean, especially as many people will use the same piece of equipment in classes. In order to absorb the shock to the head, sheets of rubber were experimentally inserted inside the *men* padding (*futon*). There have even been attempts to put little metal springs inside the *futon*, but this failed to dissipate the force of contact. To the contrary, it made the *men* more rigid and intensified the pain.

With a good quality *men* the wearer will feel no discomfort irrespective of how hard he is struck. Leaving aside existing abnormalities, receiving strikes to the head will not be detrimental to a healthy individual. Such concerns are only voiced by those who have no experiences. Those who have, immediately dispel this myth. Through my own experience, I devised the *men-shita* (under-*men*). As can be seen in ILLUSTRATION 2, the headpiece is made of cotton, and the thick padding at the top is more than enough to absorb from powerful blows to the head. The ears are also covered to protect the eardrums, but hearing is not impeded. Also, as the face and chin does not come into direct contact with the inside of the *men*, hygiene is easy to maintain.

ILLUSTRATION 2: MEN-SHITA

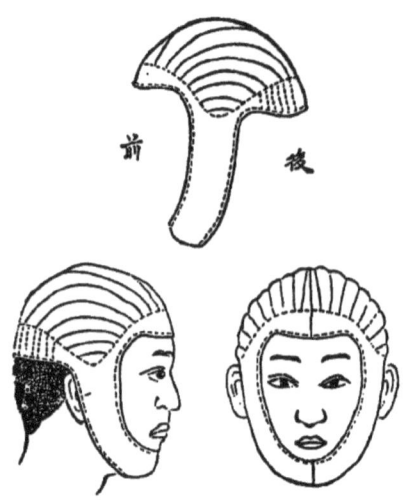

With the "*men-shita*" it is unnecessary to wrap a *tenugui* around the head, and it can conveniently be washed as many times as necessary. Using a *nodo-ate* (throat pad) will improve safety, but is certainly not requisite. The elbows can be rendered powerless if struck with wayward blow, so it is advisable to wear pads. There are many people who claim that such extra protection is pointless, and that learning to withstand some pain here and there is what makes kendo effective as a form of *shugyō* (ascetic training). This may seem a reasonable line of thought, but it is in fact mistaken.

There is little chance of a practitioner suffering a serious injury through *bōgu* imperfections, however, the unpleasant experience of pain when struck will quickly kill a novice's enthusiasm. They will feel resentful, and even those with more experience will lack drive if they are afraid of the impending discomfort. Purposefully inflicting pain is an evil act that benefits no one in terms of physical and mental growth or technical advancement.

It is uncommon for people to get injured through being struck or thrust at in training. If one happens to get injured, it is usually because they were lethargic. Somebody who is brimming with energy will not be perturbed by blows to uncovered parts of the body. This will be difficult to comprehend in the initial stages, but students should be constantly reminded that even a perfect set of *bōgu* is useless if the wearer is lacking in spirit.

To keep the equipment clean, be sure to use a *tenugui* or a *men-shita* during use, and place the *bōgu* in the sunlight in a place free of mud or dust to dry. Cover the inside of the *men* with a white cloth and every so often detach the inner part to wash. The *men-gane*, inside of the *men*, *kote* and so on can be washed with phenol water or formalin solution to disinfect it. As many students will use the same equipment, such measures are necessary to ensure that infectious diseases and dermatological infections are not transmitted. To store equipment away, tie each set up and ensure that it is able to air in a dry place. If the *bōgu* will not be used for a while during holidays or the like, take measures to prevent it going mouldy. Do not use *bōgu* that has mould without cleaning it properly first. Minor damage in equipment is easily overlooked. This can lead to more serious deterioration, resulting in blisters forming on the hands and various other problems. Remember that inadequate upkeep of equipment can cause all manner of problems later. Always maintain equipment. In particular, *shinai* are prone to splinter and can be very dangerous if not checked.

Bokutō are employed in the practice of fundamental movements. The hilt (*tsuka*) of the *shinai* is round, and the blade is straight and cylindrical, so it is not conducive to teaching how to manipulate a real sword. The *bokutō* is closer in form to a *katana* and is thus useful for imparting how to hold a sword and strike correctly with the cutting edge of the blade rather than the sides. The length of the *bokutō* is set at *3-shaku 3-sun 5-bu* (123.6cm) with the *tsuka* measuring *8-sun* (24.2cm) and *5-bu* (1.5cm) space between the *tsuba* and the *seppa*.

Section 5—Grading System

The provision of grades or ranks to gauge progress in kendo is an effective means for encouraging students, and provides many advantages from the perspective of teaching. Therefore, I am of the belief that introducing grades and examining students closely to award them is appropriate. There are many dojos and schools that already have systems in place to rate the student's technical ability. However, the criteria varies and is far from unified. Before the Meiji Restoration (1868), various martial art schools made use of terms such as *kirigami*, *mokuroku*, *menkyo* and so on to indicate the student's level of mastery in that style. Still, there was great disparity between the schools in terminology and standards. Consequently, considerable confusion arose and many problems arose in terms of abuse. The Keishichō (Metropolitan Police) introduced a grading system starting from the rank of 7-*kyū* through to 2-*kyū*. Other groups followed their lead but the judging criteria was often imprecise.

In the old days, students were never awarded a scroll of recognition until their technical ability was deemed to be good enough. Also, secret principles of the various schools were often conveyed orally with much discretion, and the knowledge was not even allowed to be disclosed to family members. This was to protect the integrity of the school of swordsmanship. Nowadays, however, there are no such things as "secret teachings" in kendo. Everything exists as public knowledge for individuals to research on their own, and this does not need to be a requirement when assessing rank. The number of ranks, what they are called, and how they are assessed can be left open to interpretation. However, as judo and kendo are already well-established in the community and promoted as national sports of Japan, it is best that the terms and criteria are consistent. In actuality, I think that the *dan-kyū* system that is being utilised in judo would be the best fit for kendo as well, which is why I have been implementing it at various institutions. The following is a comparison with the system of grades employed by the Keishichō.

There are five *kyū* grades preceeding Shodan (in kendo and judo) starting at *gokyū* through to *ikkyū*.

Keishichō	Judo (Kendo)
Gokyū (5th Kyū)	Shodan, Nidan (1st Dan, 2nd Dan)
Yonkyū (4)	Sandan, Yondan (3rd Dan, 4th Dan)
Sankyū (3)	Godan, Rokudan (5th Dan, 6th Dan)
Nikyū (2)	Nanadan, Hachidan (7th Dan, 8th Dan)

KENDO FOR ADULTS

By Hatano Toshio (Courtesy of *Kendo Nihon*)
Translated by Alex Bennett

Hatano Toshio-sensei was born in January 1945 in Musashi Murayama, Tokyo. After graduating from Kokushikan High School and Nihon University, he became a salaryman for a few years before establishing the Nanbudō Kendōgu shop in 1971. He passed the 8-dan exam on his second attempt in 1994. He serves as an advisor for the West Tokyo Kendo Federation, and is Suruga University Kendo Club Shihan, Musashi Murayama City Kendo Federation president, and leader of the Kinryūkan Dojo.

Part 4: The Importance of Kirikaeshi for Mature Practitioners

A characteristic of both *kirikaeshi* and *kakari-geiko* is that the attacker just attacks and is not concerned about being hit. In this sense, there is little danger of strange habits forming through the act of dodging incoming blows. This, I think, is where the benefits of these exercises lie.

These days, *kirikaeshi* is conducted at the beginning and end of *keiko* almost as a kind of ritual. Even though everybody acknowledges *kirikaeshi* as the most fundamental of *kihon* exercises, most people actually don't get it. Practising *kirikaeshi* leads to precision and *sae* (crispness or decisiveness) in technique, but you have to do it properly to reap the benefits. If you do it wrong, it leads to bad habits which are difficult to rectify later.

Almost all coaches of strong kendo teams say that their trainings focus on doing the basics properly. This means that you can improve your skills for *shiai* by doing lots of *kirikaeshi*. This is the approach I take when teaching at my college kendo club. If you work hard at the basics up to college level, then it is just a matter of making slight adjustments as you get older. If you don't have a firm grounding in the basics in your younger days, however, your progress will be impeded when you join the workforce and have less time to dedicate to training. It will be hard to iron out all of your idiosyncrasies, and improvement will be slow.

What are some of the points to watch out for in *kirikaeshi*? Many people do the exercise without moving their left hand. To cut, you need to move your left hand from above your head to around solar-plexus height. Moving your right hand only is incorrect, but people don't recognise this because their *kensen* is still moving. It is important to have your left hand move in a tight V-shape as you strike from side to side. The instant the *shinai* makes contact with the left and right *men*, the left hand is at the bottom of the V.

There are no benefits from practising kirikaeshi without moving the left hand up and down the vertical axis, even though you are still striking from side to side.

The left fist moves up and down. Always be conscious of this as you strike left and right men.

When I cut through bamboo with a *katana*, I found that cutting down on a diagonal from left to right was cleaner than from right to left, even though right to left seems more comfortable and easier. In other words, in the context of kendo it is more difficult to strike the opponent's right *men* (your left), but the direction of the blade (*hasuji*) is ultimately better. This discovery was very interesting to me. I deduced from this that the left hand is the key. When cutting from the upper right through to the lower left, you left side is prone to open up, however, this is not the case when cutting from the upper left down to the lower right. That is why the *hasuji* is more precise, and the cut is cleaner. In other words, if the left flank of the body is not exposed, the left hand keeps on the right trajectory without wavering.

Be sure to observe your opponent carefully when receiving *kirikaeshi*. In many cases you will notice that the left hand is in the centre when they strike your right *men*, but it veers away from the centreline when they strike your left *men*. It feels awkward to cut on a left diagonal, but as the left hand doesn't veer off in a curve away from the optimum trajectory, it results in a much cleaner cut. Thus, it is important to consciously prevent your left flank from opening up when you strike left-*men* (your right). Even high-ranking kenshi need to be careful of this.

Also, many people neglect to aim for *men*, and seem to be intent on striking the receiving *shinai* instead. I receive by guiding the attacker's strokes into the *men* and making sure the *shinai* reaches the target as if wrapping around the receiving *shinai*. This helps to

Strike with the intention of making your shinai wrap around the receiver's to land on men.

The left flank is prone to opening up when striking hidari-men.

Keep your left flank closed.

develop a crisp striking motion, as opposed to just striking the *shinai*, which makes the movement flat and restricted. If you compare this to baseball, for example, it's like a pitch that suddenly zips around the batter's hands, making it very difficult to hit. This is referred to as a "live ball". In kendo, a "live strike" is one that extends out at the precise point of impact. This can be learned by doing *kirikaeshi* properly.

If you can't do it well, I suggest that you slow things down to correct the form first. It is much better to do it slowly and accurately rather than fast and incorrectly. If you can execute *kirikaeshi* properly, this also hones the skills you need to perform techniques such as *kaeshi-waza* and *suriage-waza*. It is not easy to do *kirikaeshi* correctly, which is why instructors need to be particularly strict. Students tend to take the easy way out and fall into lazy habits. This has no merit at all.

Receiving is Study for *Tenouchi*

Once the correct movement is mastered, it is important to keep doing the routine until becoming a little fatigued. Go until you feel you have no more energy to strike, otherwise you will not gain anything from the exercise. When you start out, your strikes will be powerful, but this strength will dissipate as you keep going. This is what you are aiming for. *Kirikaeshi* is not a warmup exercise. I get my students to repeat *kirikaeshi* over and over. I have to remind them that I am not doing it to make their lives miserable, but because the benefits to be had by doing it correctly are immense. I make a point of praising them when they learn to strike without excess power.

An important factor in doing *kirikaeshi* correctly is to receive the right way. From *chūdan*, raise the *kensen* without shifting the position of the left hand. Try to keep the *kensen* in this position without moving it from the centre, and alternate the left hand from left to right as you receive. Tighten your grip with each strike, as if you are deflecting the strike down (*uchi-otoshi*). This will teach you the best way to manipulate the power in your hands and fingers (*tenouchi*) for executing *ōji-waza*. In this way, the receiver must also learn from the exercise.

A lot of people can be seen receiving with their left arm bent at the elbow, but this is not correct. This method of receiving is useful when training with more advanced practitioners, but is not suitable when teaching beginners. Deflecting their *shinai* down as if you are executing *ōji-waza* will stifle their strikes, and they will not get the extra stretch that they need at the end. Instead, for beginners you should receive by using your *shinai* to guide or pull their strikes into *men*. When alternating your *shinai* from left to right, rather than being vertical, the *kensen* should be leaning in towards you and on a slight angle on each side, like a partially open umbrella. This will enable the attacker to follow through with each strike rather than stopping it dead in its tracks. If the receiver is bad, the attacker will have a hard time doing it properly.

Learning to Breathe in *Kirikaeshi* Extends to the *Seme-ai*

Kirikaeshi is usually done with four forward strikes and five going back, but this was not originally the case. In the old days, there was no set number of strikes, and you had to keep going until your sensei decided it was okay to stop. This was usually after exhaustion had set in, and you were striking with no excess strength.

The *kirikaeshi* routine that is commonly practised today should be done with one breath or as few breaths as possible. The strikes should be big, and the wrists turned and stretched fully on each cut with the intention of hitting *men*. I suspect that the four-forward five-backward method became entrenched because nine strikes is about as long as one can go with one breath. To last the distance, exhale a little at a time as you strike. This is achieved by shouting as you strike but attempting not to exhale. This is difficult for beginners, and it is okay to take a breath half way through, but they should keep persevering until they can do one sequence of nine strikes in one breath.

Receiving is important. To guide the attacker's shinai in, have the kensen of your shinai angled slightly inwards.

When receiving for a beginner, pull your shinai in towards your body.

Add more resistance to the block when receiving for more advanced practitioners.

Then, there is the final strike to *shōmen*. After making the ninth strike to left-*men* (striker's right) and retreating, keep extending your breath while directing your *kensen* to the centreline, and then launch in for the final strike. Many people drop their *shinai* after the ninth, and breathe in before making the final strike. Instructors fail to point this out. It is the most excruciating part of the sequence, but you must keep the connection unbroken.

There are several benefits to be gained from learning to extend your exhalation. You cannot move swiftly or freely as you inhale. When you strike *debana-kote* or *debana-men*, you have to be exhaling for the technique to succeed in terms of timing. When facing off against an opponent from the *issoku-ittō* interval, try to inhale in short sharp bursts and exhale slowly for as long as possible. From this position, put pressure on and assail your opponent (*seme-ai*). As you get closer, you will start to run out of breath, and it gets painful. If you can't resist the urge to take a breath here, you will miss the opportunity to strike when your opponent moves, and you may be struck instead. At such a time, it is best to move out of striking distance, take a breath, and start again.

They may or may not be conscious of it, but when a strong kenshi scores a point, this is what is usually happening with their breathing. *Kirikaeshi* is the best way to learn to breathe properly in kendo regardless of rank.

Zeami, the famous Noh theatre master, wrote of the "flower of the moment" in his treatise *Fūsei Kaden*. Those in their teens, twenties, thirties and so on all have their own flowers appropriate to their age. This means that an art can be pursued for a lifetime, and each age has its own point of beauty that is aspired to. This includes people in their forties, fifties, and sixties. Zeami said that an actor who was good in his youth but not so in his later years has lost sight

When retreating after the ninth strike, keep exhaling and then strike the final shōmen without taking a breath.

of his flower, and has forgotten how to bloom. An actor who blossoms throughout his career is able to do so because he has "something special" within. He is always seeking and striving to reach a higher plane.

Kendo is exactly the same. Some people develop a presence or "something special" as they get older. In years gone by at the Kyoto Taikai, who could not be utterly moved by the demonstration matches of Nakakura Kiyoshi-sensei and Morishima Tateo-sensei, men both in their eighties? It is not surprising that a special aura emanated from these men the moment they took *kamae*, given their years of hard training and constant pursuit of a higher understanding of kendo. Morishima-sensei was particularly famous for the emphasis he placed on *kirikaeshi* and *kakari-geiko*.

The Way of Kendo;
      Tirelessly, perseveringly, take your time.

Hatano Hitoshi's Comments

Morishima-sensei is the Shihan of Meiji University's kendo club. When I was a student there, the first hour of training was *kirikaeshi*, and the second hour was *kakari-geiko*. That was all we did. Even though Morishima-sensei always put on his gear on, often we never did any *jigeiko*. Even if we did get to do *jigeiko*, it was after we were completely exhausted through *kirikaeshi* and *kakari-geiko*. It was tough, but the members learned to relax and remove unnecessary strength from their strikes. Many top level high school students were recruited into the Meiji University kendo club, but everybody's kendo was ultimately transformed by Morishima-sensei, and his hard training methods gave incredible substance to our *kamae* and manner.

Hatano Hitoshi

38 years old. Hatano-sensei's son. Works for a dispatch company called Bstyle. Studied under H8-dan Morishima Tateo-sensei. Had a ten-year break from kendo, but now trains once or twice a week after work.

Uncle Kotay's Kendo Korner

Part 2: the pleats in the hakama

Q: Uncle Kotay, what do the pleats in the hakama mean? They're a pain in the neck to keep straight and creased. What's the point anyway? (#pleatpolice)

A: A good question lad. Many people out there in Kendo Land are probably not aware of the meaning behind the pleats, or why we even wear *hakama* in kendo anyway. Apart from the obvious advantages of having cool air blowing up your legs and into your nether regions in the stinking hot summer months, the *hakama* is a strange piece of apparel that has been around a lot longer than flared jeans. Many centuries in fact, and there have been different styles in vogue throughout the ages. The type we use in kendo today with the *koshi-ita* board in the small of the back was first worn by samurai around the end of the sixteenth century. They were comfortable to wear when riding horses, easy to relieve yourself, and don't chafe when walking long distances! They were also pretty useful for hiding tell-tale footwork when fencing in the dojo. Practical and chic at the same time.

As for the pleats, well it's hard to know exactly why they became a thing. After all, does anybody know why trousers have creases in the front and back? Part of it is surely connected with fashion sense, but standard theory today is that the five pleats at the front of the *hakama* represent the Confucian ideals of "*gorin-gojō*". That means the "five Confucian filial-piety relationships" of ruler to ruled, father to son, husband to wife, elder brother to younger brother, friend to friend, and/or the "five cardinal Confucian virtues" of justice (*gi*), politeness (*rei*), wisdom (*chi*), fidelity (*chu*), and benevolence (*jin*). Then there is the single crease on the back of the *hakama* which corresponds to the virtue of sincerity (*makoto*). There are no historical documents that can corroborate this theory, but it sure does sound viable. Besides, it has become firmly entrenched as kendo lore so that's the way it is now.

From a more practical perspective the pleats also offer a certain degree of protection from wayward strikes to the lower body. The loose space at the front absorbs the blows making it far less painful than if wearing tightfitting trousers.

So, when you fold your *hakama* try to remember each of the virtues as you fold the creases one by one. That way, your *hakama* will be neat and tidy, and it is an opportunity to reflect on the profound philosophical aspects of kendo as a way for personal development. In the context of kendo, dishevelled *hakama* means bedraggled brain and slipshod personality, so be sure to keep the pleats creased. That means taking the time to fold your *hakama* carefully after each training instead of rolling it into a ball and stuffing it in your bag. Tidy, shipshape pleats pumpkins. They've gotta be good for you!

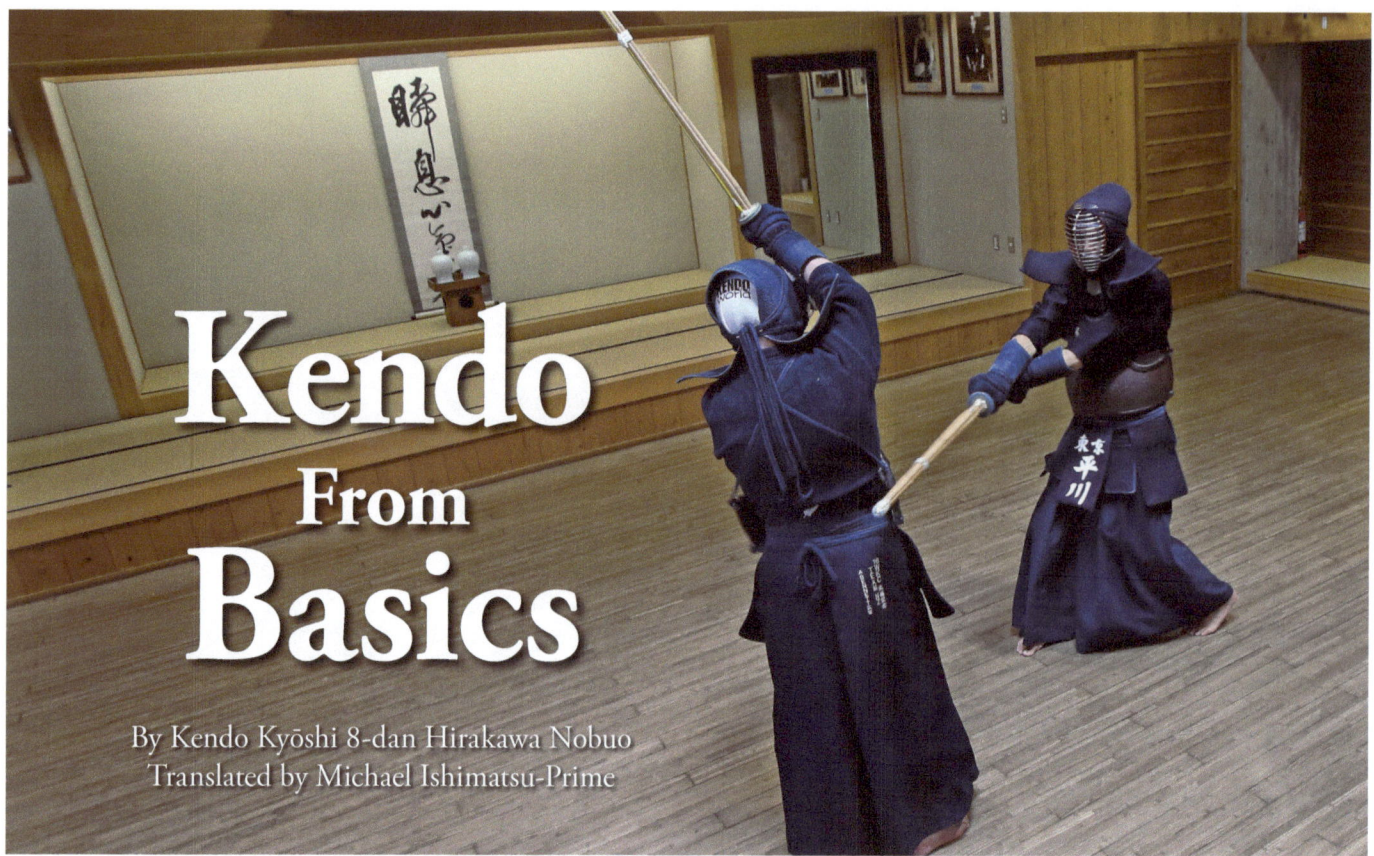

Kendo From Basics

By Kendo Kyōshi 8-dan Hirakawa Nobuo
Translated by Michael Ishimatsu-Prime

Hirakawa Nobuo-sensei's *Kendo From Basics* was originally published in 1993. It proved to be very popular and went through several printings in the original Japanese. Chinese and Korean language translations have also been made, and now, *Kendo World* has translated it into English and will publish it in 2016.

As the title of the book suggests, it starts with a discussion of the basics. This includes explanations of *shizentai*, *rei*, *kamae*, *ashi-sabaki*, and basic strikes and how to receive them. These are then used as the base for very detailed examinations of *uchi-otoshi-waza*, *harai-waza*, *tsubazeriai-waza*, *katsugi-waza*, *kaeshi-waza*, *nuki-waza*, *suriage-waza*, *osae-waza*, *maki-waza*, and *jōdan-waza* in the Applied Techniques chapter.

The *Kendo World* team spent a few days in summer and winter 2015 with Hirakawa-sensei at Noma Dojo in Tokyo retaking all the photos. Unlike the original Japanese edition, the *Kendo World* version will be full colour and also available in the Zinio ebook format. As a preview, here is a section from the Applied Techniques chapter.

Applied Techniques
Creating a debana striking opportunity

1. Move the tip of the *shinai* out of the way to invite an attack

Being full of spirit and without showing any will to retreat, apply pressure on the opponent little by little. Quickly move the tip of the *shinai* away from the centreline towards the left chest area of your opponent, thereby creating an opening for them to strike. When your opponent comes in to attack, immediately strike *men* or *kote*.

Important Points
- Engage in sync (*aiki*) with your opponent and then momentarily change the rhythm.
- Apply pressure with feeling and creep forward from the toes into *uchima*.
- Do not strike with just the hands. Strike with the intent of breaking the opponent's centre with your whole body.
- When shifting the tip of the *shinai* away from the centreline, take care not to move it outside the opponent's bodyline.

Attacking men

Attacking kote

Attacking right-kote	*Attacking right-dō*	*Attacking right-men*

2. Stepping forward and backward to make an opponent attack

Repeatedly step forward and back; then while stepping back, slightly lower the tip of the *shinai* to invite an attack. Just as the opponent starts to attack, strike centre-*men* or left or right *men*.

Important Points
- When moving forward or backward, don't think about blocking their attack. You must always be ready to strike.
- When moving back and dropping the tip of the *shinai* to invite an attack, practise moving the left foot diagonally back to the left or right pointing in the direction of the opponent's centreline, and strike the moment the opponent moves to attack.
- When moving back, do not move the left foot back but pull the right foot in (*tsugi-ashi*) to "steal the *maai*" and strike at the moment the opponent moves to attack.
- To create an opening, move forward and back with footwork like that used in *choyaku-suburi*, kicking slightly with the left foot.

3. Make your opponent attack by moving diagonally left and right, forward and back

Move freely to the forward and back to the diagonal left and right, striking the instant your opponent moves.

Important Points
- Keep the arms relaxed and manoeuvre from the hips. Always let the opponent take the centre to create an opening for *debana*.
- Refrain from moving with the same rhythm all of the time.

Attacking centre-men from the omote side

▼

▼

▼

▼

▼

THE GREATER MEANING OF KENDO

REI DAN JI CHI

REIDAN-JICHI PART 21

Hiki-waza

By Prof. Ōya Minoru (Kendo Kyōshi 7-dan)
International Budo University

Translated by Alex Bennett

Hiki-waza are techniques executed after a body clash (*taiatari*), from *tsuba-zeriai*, or from close in. Techniques are struck while going backwards. Therefore, the attacker has to consciously create openings to strike by unsettling the opponent's *kamae* or hand position.

(1) Breaking the Opponent's *Kamae*

Breaking the opponent's *kamae* is called *kuzushi*. To strike *hiki-waza* you first have to unsettle the opponent and take advantage of their reaction and resulting openings by going straight back or to the diagonal rear.

1. From *Taiatari*

The momentum continues after making a strike, the hands are lowered to the abdominal area with the *shinai* held vertically, and the body smashes into the opponent to knock them off balance.

2. Left or Right *Kuzushi*

- Turning your body to the left, use the left hand to push the opponent's right elbow from the side.
- Turn your body to the right and use your right hand to push the opponent's left elbow from the side.

3. Back or Forward *Kuzushi*

- Use the left hand to bump the opponent's left hand up. The opponent will respond by pushing down.
- Use the right hand to knock the opponent's right hand down. The opponent will push back up.
- Push the opponent strongly. The opponent will react by pushing back.

(2) Things to Consider for *Hiki-waza*

The three targets for *hiki-waza* are *kote*, *men*, and *dō*. In recent years, when striking from *tsubazeriai* many people move the upper body back first and then catch their balance and propel themselves back by kicking

Kuzushi with taiatari	Moving straight back	Men
	Moving back to diagonal right	
Left and right kuzushi	Moving back to diagonal left	
	Moving back to diagonal left	Kote
Back or forward kuzushi	Moving straight back	Dō
	Moving back to diagonal left	

off with the front foot as they strike. This method runs counter to the principles of footwork and *shinai* use. It might seem as though this method is faster, but this is an illusion. Those striking will actually render themselves unbalanced and susceptible to attack while retreating.

The basic movement for *hiki-waza* is exactly the same as the motion in *suburi*. In other words, when moving forward the right foot steps out as the *shinai* is lifted overhead, and the left foot is drawn up as the *shinai* is brought down for the strike. The opposite is the case for striking backward, and this is how *hiki-waza* is executed. That is, stepping back with the left foot as the *shinai* is lifted overhead, and drawing the right foot back to the left as the strike is made. This method ensures overall stability and striking with correct *hasuji* (trajectory). Retreating with *okuri-ashi* enables quick transition to the next technique if required. This is the correct way to execute *hiki-waza*.

(3) Waza

1. *Hiki-men*
a. When the opponent pushes back – Use the power from the opponent's reactionary push-back, take a large step to the rear from the left foot as the *shinai* is swung overhead, and snap the right foot back to the left as the strike is made.
b. When the opponent pushes your *shinai* to the right – If the opponent pushes your *shinai* to the right, instantaneously disengage by lifting the *shinai* overhead while taking a large step back to the diagonal left from the left foot, and snap the right foot back to the left as the strike is made.

2. *Hiki-kote*
While taking a large step back to the diagonal left from the left foot, push the opponent's right elbow from the side with the left hand to unbalance them, and snap the right foot back to the left foot as you strike *kote*.

3. *Hiki-dō*
Push the opponent's left hand up with your left fist while taking a large backward step from the left foot and strike *dō* as the right foot is snapped back to the left foot.

<Important Points>
- Be sure to identify when the opponent's posture is unbalanced and the way they react to pushes.
- Use your lower back for power when breaking your opponent's posture.
- The footwork for *hiki-waza* requires taking a large rearward step from the left foot, and immediately snapping the right foot back at the same time as the strike.
- Manoeuvre your body so that you are striking your opponent from a front-on position.
- When retreating after the strike, never turn your back to the opponent. Keep them in your sights from a front-on position while moving back and be sure that your *kensen* is pointing to their centreline to thwart any follow-up attack.
- When stepping back to the diagonal rear, be sure to keep your body front-on *vis-à-vis* the opponent, and turn your wrists sufficiently as you strike to ensure the blade trajectory is correct.

"Geisha no kokoro sutetsubeshi"
(Discard the mind of artistry...)

Odagiri Ichiun (1630–1706). Sekiun's number one disciple in the Mujūshin-ryū.

"Those who study this school must discard the mind of an artist, and not turn the science of military strategy into a commodity."

Ichiun hailed from the province of Aizu. He had aspirations of becoming a physician, but was also an aficionado of the martial arts. When he was 27 or 28 years of age, he became a disciple of Harigaya Sekiun. In fact, it was because of his learned student's writings that Sekiun's teachings and style of *kenjutsu* became famous. In particular, Ichiun's books *Sekiun-ryū kenjutsu-sho* and *Tenshin dokuro* were very well known.

Legend has it that they met when Ichiun asked Sekiun to make him a wooden sword with a metal bar embedded within. Apparently, Ichiun had killed a known bully in a duel, and was convinced that the man's family wanted to exact revenge. Ichiun needed to defend himself, but wanted to take life no more. It seems Sekiun, apart from being a skilled swordsman, was also quite handy at carving things out of wood.

One thing led to another, and before long Ichiun was studying the "Sword of the Non-Abiding Mind" under Sekiun. For five years, Ichiun applied himself in his studies, and when he felt he had learned the inner secrets, he challenged his master to three bouts. Each one ended in "*ai-nuke*", in which both "passed through" unscathed. Sekiun rewarded him with a scroll of mastery.

Sekiun died three years later at the age of 70, at which time Ichiun hung up his swords and dedicated his time to studying Zen. Through popular demand,

SWORDS OF WISDOM

By
ALEX BENNETT
Based on the book
"KENSHI NO MEIGON" (1998)
by the late Tobe Shinjūrō
Used with author's permission.

however, he was coaxed out of retirement to teach hankering warriors who wanted access to his legendary knowledge. When word got out that Ichiun was back in the game, many came to seek his instruction. Although the Mujūshin-ryū's philosophy decried the idea of amassing fame and fortune through the vehicle of violence, some of his new charges were more than prepared to benefit from their association with the school. In other words, their primary objective was to sell their art, which was in violation of the spirit of the school's teachings.

Ichiun was well aware of this tendency in some of his students and admonished them. "Those who study this school must discard the mind of an artist, and not turn the science of military strategy into a commodity." In other words, use of the term "artist" here implies that student must avoid becoming an expert of martial performance for personal gain. To him, the science of martial strategy was a Way, and its study was for the pursuit of a higher attainment of humanly virtue. His ideals were the exception rather than the norm, and many of his contemporaries were more intent on creating a niche for themselves in the prestigious and lucrative martial market. To many, it was about honour and profit.

Disappointed with the way the school's teachings were being exploited, Ichiun once again decided to hang up his swords and lead the life of a recluse. But his uncanny awareness of the evil intent of others never lost its edge. A would-be assassin crept into his chamber when Ichiun was fast asleep and was about to do the dastardly deed when Ichiun suddenly asked him, "What the hell do you think you're doing?" The assassin stopped in his tracks, then Ichiun rolled over and went back to sleep. The assassin left knowing that there were no openings for him to strike. Best let sleeping dogs lie, 'cos they still bite…

Another time, a young samurai came calling and confronted Ichiun, saying, "I have heard rumours that a strike by your *shinai* is too hard to withstand. If this is so, I wish to experience it first-hand. Hit me with your rhythm stick. Hit me." Ichiun complied and bopped him on his *kabuto*-protected noggin. It was a stupid thing to request, and the silly fellow staggered off behind a persimmon tree to vomit blood.

At least he wasn't killed by Ichiun. This would also have run counter to the school's philosophy of giving up the desire for fame or gain and self-glorification, and even the desire for victory. He taught people to give up all material attachments in order to travel the path of enlightenment and peace. In Ichiun's words, as quoted by legendary Zen scholar Daisetz Suzuki:

"The perfect swordsman avoids quarrelling or fighting. Fighting means killing. How can one human being bring himself to kill a fellow being? We are all meant to love, not kill, one another. It is abhorrent that one should be thinking all the time of fighting and coming out victorious. We are moral beings, we are not to lower ourselves to the status of animal. What is the use of becoming a fine swordsman if one loses his human dignity? The best thing is to be a victor without fighting."

The Life of Hayashizaki Jinsuke Minamoto no Shigenobu

By Jack James

During the Muromachi period (1333–1573) lived a man who would go on to change the art of swordsmanship forever. The legacy he left has survived nearly half a millennium.

On January 12, 1542, a boy named Asano Tamijimaru was born into a warrior family in Hayashizaki village, Tateyama, Dewane no Kuni (modern-day Murayama city, Yamagata prefecture). His father was Asano Kazuma no Minamoto Shigenari, a retainer to the Mogami clan in charge of the south-eastern part of Dewa. He served Mogami Inaba-no-Kami Mitsuhide, the sixth Mogami lord and the fifteenth lord of Tateoka castle in the Kitamurayama district of Tateoka city (modern-day Tateoka in Murayama city, Yamagata prefecture). Asano was known as a gentle and outgoing individual, earning him the trust of his lord.

Tamijimaru's mother, Sugano, was the daughter of the Takamori household in Tateoka. She was once a handmaiden to the princess of Yamagata Kasumi castle, and was an intelligent woman with a strong sense of determination, excelling in many arts.

At the age of five[1] Tamijimaru's family was struck by tragedy. In 1547 Tamijimaru's father was murdered by Sakagami Shuzen (also known as Ichiunsai or Sakagawa Unsai) a fellow retainer of the Mogami clan. Serving as a martial art instructor to the clan, Sakagawa bore a strong grudge and sense of envy toward Asano, due to the way he performed etiquette within the castle. One night, blinded by his resentment, Sakagawa ambushed Asano on his way back from visiting his family grave at Hayashizaki Myōjin Shrine. Sakagawa killed him and fled into the dead of night.

Tamijimaru and his mother Sugano, deprived of their rice winner, were thrown into utter poverty. It is said that from the moment his father was murdered, his mother spent years praying to the deity of Hayashizaki Daimyōjin Shrine with a single wish—vengeance for her husband's death. With infant in her arms, Sugano prayed every day at the shrine, all the while waiting for her son to come of age, and enact her husband's vengeance. Learning from his mother that his father was murdered by a man called Sakagawa Shuzen, Tamijimaru took his first step onto the long path of vengeance, and began his martial arts training as his mother instructed.

When he reached the age of seven, Tamijimaru began studying Kyō-ryū Kenjutsu Heihō under Higashine

---

[1] Many sources cite Hayashizaki's age as six, and subsequent ages a year older. This is due to the *kazoedoshi* tradition in Japan of being classed a one-year-old at birth, and ageing one year at the New Year.

Jirō Dayū, a chief vassal and *kenjutsu* instructor to the Mogami clan. The famed Yoshioka brothers whom Miyamoto Musashi defeated were said to be practitioners of this school.

Aged 12, Tamijimaru decided to retire to Hayashizaki Daimyōjin to begin training in earnest. However, his spirit and technique were not one, and he developed very little during this time.

When he was 14 years old, Tamijimaru went once more to the shrine to perform 100 days of prayer, this time pouring his entire soul into his training. On this occasion his dedication shone through, with his spirit and technique harmonising. One night, the deity of the shrine appeared to him in his dreams. Tamijimaru received the innermost secrets of swordsmanship from the deity. It was at this moment that his sword became one with a divine power; a supreme form of *battōjutsu* (drawing the blade and cutting) was born, and was destined to shine throughout history.

This was the birth of Musō Shinden Jūshin-ryū. It is not known when Tamijimaru started to use the Jūshin-ryū or Musō Shinden-ryū name, but he was calling his school Musō Shinden by the time he welcomed his first disciple.

Among the secrets of *battō* bestowed to Tamijimaru was "*kesa no hitotachi no seishin*".

"Do not draw, do not force others to draw. Do not cut, do not force others to cut. Do not kill, do not be killed. Even if one encounters the greatest of sinners, one should kindly offer sermon and show them the path of good men. If the worst occurs and they do not conform, then without hesitation apply *kesauchi* and send them to Buddha."[2]

It taught the young Tamijimaru that one should avoid violence at all costs, and instead aim to steer the opponent onto the righteous path of peace and morality. He learnt that it was better to create a great man who in turn would create more great men, instead of just killing. It was only as a last resort that one should use force, and this was to prevent others from being subsequently killed by that man. This was known as "*katsujinken*"—the life-giving sword.

In order to attain this state, Tamijimaru would have to cut away the "three poisons" from within: *don*, *shin* and *chi*. "*Don*" refers to the Buddhist *rāga* or desire, "*shin*" to *dvesa* or rage, and lastly "*chi*" being *moha* or ignorance. After detaching himself from these poisons he finally achieved serenity, thus wielding a "sword of compassion", and represented the god of the shrine itself.

He also received the secrets of the "*sanjaku sanzun katana*" (a one-metre long sword) and "*kyūsun gobu wakizashi*" (approx. 29cm short sword) with the techniques of "*manjinuki*", the ability to instantly draw the long sword using the left and right hand in perfect harmony.[3] One should use the long sword as if it were short, and the short sword as if it were long. "Destroy your opponent's distance and timing by smothering them, but still be able to draw the long sword. Also be able to overcome tremendous distance utilising every inch of one's body and the short sword."

Upon reaching the age of 17 in 1559, Asano Tamijimaru changed his name after discovering his new self, a practice very common for Japanese warriors. He henceforth went by the name of Hayashizaki Jinsuke Shigenobu. He chose Hayashizaki after the name of his village, Jinsuke after his father's infant name, and Shigenobu by utilising the first character of his father Shigenari's name.

Soon after this, Hayashizaki Jinsuke Shigenobu was taught the inner secrets of Kyō-ryū Kenjutsu Heihō from Higashine Jirō Dayū. He travelled back to the

---

2 More information on the linguistic side of "Kesa no Hitotachi no Seishin" by the author can be found here: https://jushinden.wordpress.com/2013/04/25/kesa-no-hitotachi-no-seishin/

3 Many sources claim he mastered the secret of utilising a long hilt for *iai* but this is incorrect. The mistake was born from Higashi Shimano-no-Kami Motoharu having a student of a student with a similar name: Hayashizaki Jinsuke Katsuyoshi. He was a practitioner of Shintō-ryū *kenjutsu* which purports the benefits of a longer sword and hilt. Tamijimaru inherited the secrets of the longer sword, and the hilt was longer simply for balance. His focus was on instantaneous reaction from the scabbard. Tamiya Heibei no Jō Shigemasa was also a practitioner adept with a sword with a long *tsuka* to gain distance over the opponent (but not a longer sword).

shrine where he received his epiphany, and vowed to the deity that he still needed to right a grievous wrong and was obligated to avenge his father's death. He prayed for success on his coming journey. He requested leave from his mother and his teacher to begin *musha shugyō*—a warrior pilgrimage—and set out on what would later be known as the Nakasendō road in search of vengeance.

While walking the Nakasendō, Hayashizaki found himself in Shinshū (modern-day Nagano prefecture). He lodged at the residence of Kitayama Hanzaemon, a member of a powerful local clan. During his stay, however, the Ibara-gumi, a group of rustic samurai turned bandits, attacked the residence. In an incredible feat, Hayashizaki drew his sword and in one swift, continuous movement dispatched the leader in a flash, and easily finished off the remaining enemies. Word of this amazing act spread like wildfire. Warriors were so impressed that many requested to become his students.

After his stay in Shinshū he headed south on the Tōkaidō road in the direction of Bishū (modern-day Nagoya) where eventually he reached the castle grounds. After Bishū, he settled in the capital city, Kyoto. Along the way on his journey he trained with a number of skilled martial artists and attracted numerous disciples who would subsequently go on to create their own schools of swordsmanship.

In April of 1561, Hayashizaki took part in a martial arts competition held before the thirteenth shogun of the Ashikaga shogunate, Ashikaga Yoshiteru. Among the spectators were several local *daimyō* warlords, including Matsunaga Tanjō. Hayashizaki spectacularly defeated Nitta Yoshiaki, a master of Shuhō-ryū, and was awarded a famous sword made by the Nobukuni family of swordsmiths. This event was another turning point for Hayashizaki's style, and further added to his already growing reputation.

Not long after his success, Hayashizaki's life took a dramatic turn of events. In May of the same year, he learned that the man who murdered his father, Sakagami Shuzen, whom he had been so desperately searching for, was living in Fushimi, Kyoto. He was hiding under the alias Rozan Daizen Toshitaka. He immediately went to see Matsunaga Tanjō whom he had met at the competition the previous month. Matsunaga was acting as the shogunate's local security officer. He was able to acquaint Hayashizaki with Miyoshi Nagayoshi, the *daimyō* holding authority over the region. His authorisation would be essential for Hayashizaki to carry out his mission. Impressed by Hayashizaki's dedication to his father, and by his martial prowess, Miyoshi gave his official approval for enact vengeance.

Filled with anticipation and determination, Hayashizaki began his reconnaissance on Sakagawa, carefully observing his movements and awaiting the opportune moment to take justice. After 11 long years, Hayashizaki confronted his father's killer at Tanbakaidō on May 17, 1561.

Drawing his Nobukuni blade, Hayashizaki clove Sakagami's head clean from his shoulders, "sending him to Buddha", in a perfect embodiment of *iai*. At last, Hayashizaki was able to put an end to his family's years of grief. After performing the Buddhist rites, Hayashizaki prepared Sakagami's head and set off on the journey back to his hometown. Almost immediately, ripples were felt through Kyoto as the story of Hayashizaki's successful revenge echoed through the streets.

Upon arriving back in his hometown, Hayashizaki told his mother and teacher of his achievement, and then lay Sakagami's head atop his father's grave. He prayed that his father could finally rest in peace, and went once more to the shrine where it all started. The local village held a festival in his honour to celebrate his martial prowess. With his mission now complete, Hayashizaki offered his Nobukuni sword to the shrine, where it is said to remain to this day.

After many years of hardship Hayashizaki's mother passed away the following year in 1562 due to illness. With no more reason to stay in Hayashizaki and keen to further improve his swordsmanship, he set out again on his second pilgrimage.

Hayashizaki headed south to Yonezawa. He took up

Shin Muso Hayashizaki-ryu Iaijutsu

residence in Akai village, Wakamatsu, spending a total of three years in southern Tōhoku. Hayashizaki took on a number of students from the surrounding area and trained them in *iai*.

In 1565, Hayashizaki travelled further south into the Kantō region, and to Kashima where he studied Tenshinshō-den Katori Shintō-ryū for around three years before setting off for his next destination. During this time, Tsukahara Bokuden was also studying the same style from his adopted father.

At age 26, Hayashizaki took up residence with Matsuda Norihide, a direct vassal of the Hōjō clan. He instructed the clansmen in the martial art he had spent years refining. The following year in 1569, Takeda Shingen's forces attacked Suruga (modern-day Shizuoka prefecture) storming Kanbara castle. Under the service of Matsuda, Hayashizaki took part in the subsequent battle. Despite massive losses to both sides, Hayashizaki demonstrated his phenomenal skill, and following the battle he presented two heads he claimed from Shingen forces. He received a direct invitation from the Hōjō clan to continue instructing martial arts to their warriors.

On May 10, 1595, Hayashizaki continued on his path south to Ichinomiya (modern-day Ōmiya, Saitama prefecture). He lived on the grounds of the local shrine for a total of three years developing his art and searching for internal harmony. After many years of wandering, he found himself in Kawagoe city on February 18, 1616, where he stayed with Takamatsu Kanbei.

The following year he departed from Kawagoe. Heading in the direction of his home village, he vanished into the sands of time. His whereabouts after this period, his place of death and location of his grave are unknown, though a humble wooden plaque remains in Kawagoe, signifying his last known abode.

It is rare for someone with as much influence as Hayashizaki to have so little recorded about him. His life and legacy took place amongst a long period of civil upheaval: the fall of the Ashikaga shogunate and a move towards decentralised government and the *daimyō* system, which subsequently cast Japan into the Warring States period. Finally, the country would arrive into a time of national unification and peace, the Edo period (1603–1868). It is thought most records were destroyed in the turmoil. Along with the death of his disciples in battle, many records were simply lost when they changed hands. Despite this, he amassed a large number of students who would continue his tradition and go on to create their own fighting methods.

Some of his notable students include the following:

- Takamatsu Kanbei Nobukatsu, Ichimiya-ryū (Takamatsu Kei)
- Higashi Shimano no Kami Motoharu, founder of Shinmyō Musō Higashi-ryū
- Tamiya Heibei no Jō Shigemasa, founder of Tamiya-ryū and second generation Jūshin-ryū
- Nagano Muraku Nyūdō Kinrosai, founder of Muraku-ryū and third generation Jūshin-ryū
- Ichimiya Sadayū Terunobu Kōshin, founder of Ichimiya-ryū, fourth generation Hayashizaki Shin Musō-ryū (Ichimiya-ryū Tani-ha)
- Sekiguchi Yarokuemon Shinshin Ujimune, founder of Sekiguchi-ryū
- Katayama Hōki no Kami Hisayasu, founder of Hōki-ryū
- Sakurai Gorōzaemon Naomitsu, teacher of Mima Yoichizaemon Kagenobu, founder of Suiō-ryū
- Ashikaga Shōgun Yoshiteru
- Hōjō Ujinao
- Date Chikuzen
- Katakura Kojūrō
- Uesugi Kagekatsu
- Iwanari Chikaranosuke
- Takikawa Sakon
- Senshi Yamashiro no Kami
- Nitta Ichirō
- Sakuraba Hayato
- Matsuda Samanosuke
- Daitōji Suruga no Kami Masashige
- Amakasu Ōmi no Kami
- Utsunomiya Mikawa no Kami
- Nagano Shinano no Kami
- Matsudaira Shuzen
- Okudaira Kuhachirō
- Torii Hikoemon

The style of swordsmanship passed on to a boy of only fourteen has continued for over 450 years, and still prospers to this day. No one knows exactly why the deity Hayashizaki Myōjin chose a young boy to receive the secrets of his divine swordsmanship. Perhaps it was a moment of compassion by the deity, looking down on a boy struggling to survive with his mother. Or, possibly Tamijimaru was destined to be an instrument through which *iaijutsu* could prosper. The only thing that is certain is that mere men will never understand the workings of the gods.

Timeline of Hayashizaki Jinsuke Minamoto-no-Shigenobu's life:

1540: Parents Asano Kazuma no Minamoto Shigenari and Sugano were married
1542: Born on January 12
1547: Father murdered by Sakagami Shuzen
1549: Entered into Higashine Dōjō to study Kyō-ryū
1554: Prayed at Hayashizaki Myōjin to improve swordsmanship, mind and technique were not ready
1556: Performed hundred-day prayer at Hayashizaki Myōjin and this time received the secrets of *iai* in an epiphany
1559: Changes name to Hayashizaki Jinsuke Shigenobu. Masters Kyō-ryū, sets out on *musha shugyō*
1560: Arrives in Kyoto

- —Awarded Nobukuni sword
- —Defeats Sakagami Shuzen at Tanbakaidō

1562: Loses his mother Sugano to illness, sets out on second pilgrimage

1563: Travels from Yonezawa and recruits students at Akai village in Wakamatsu, Aizu

1565: Studies Tenshinshō Shintō-ryū alongside Tsukahara Bokuden

1568: Enters into the service of the Hōjō Clan as a martial arts instructor

1569: Fights in the battle of Kanbara Castle

1595: Settles onto sacred grounds in Ichinomiya

1598: Leaves Ichinomiya to continue on pilgrimage

1616: Stays with Takamatsu Kanbei in Kawagoe

1617: Sets off on final journey back to his hometown, never to be heard of again

Author's postscript:

Great care and attention has been paid to make this article as historically accurate as possible, cross-referencing the dates of Hayashizaki's life across numerous sources, as well as researching the historical events happening at the same time.

Sadly, however, his life is shrouded in mystery, and inconsistencies in the story abound including different birthplaces, ages, times of various events and conflicting information on his students. Despite this, I believe this article is currently the most detailed and accurate account of his life in the English language.

Reference Material:

- Hayashizaki Jinsuke Minamoto no Shigenobu Kō Shiryo Kenkyū Iinkai 林崎甚助源重信公資料研究委員会. *Hayashizaki Myōjin to Hayashizaki Jinsuke Shigenobu* 林崎明神と林崎甚助重信. Murayama 村山市: Hayashizaki Jinsuke Minamoto no Shigenobu Kō Shiryo Kenkyū Iinkai 出版社: 林崎甚助源重信公資料研究委員会, 2014.
- Kimura Eiju 木村榮壽. *Hayashizaki Battōjutsu Heihō Musō Shinden Jūshin-ryū* 林崎抜刀術兵法 夢想神傳重信流伝書集及び業手付解説. Hōfu 防府市: Kimura Shigeki 木村茂喜, 1981.
- Ono Renzan 小野蓮山. *Ten no Tsurugi* 天の剣. Hirosaki 弘前市: Nakamura Hideo 中村秀雄, 1993.
- Tsumaki Seirin 妻木正鱗. *Yōkai Tamiya-ryū Iai* 詳解 田宮流居合. Tokyo 東京都: Ski Journal Co., Ltd. 株式会社スキージャーナル, 1991.
- Masaoka Kazutane 政岡壹實. *Musō Jikiden Eishin Ryū Iai Heihō Chi no Maki* 無双直伝英信流居合兵法地之巻: Musō Jikiden Eishin Ryū Iai Heihō Ōe Ha Kotōkai Headquarters, 無双直伝英信流居合兵法大江派湖刀会本部, 1974.
- Yamakoshi Masaki 山越正樹. *Kyōto Yamauchi Ha Musō Jikiden Eishin-ryū Iaijutsu* 京都山内派無雙直傳英信流居合術. Kyoto 京都府: Eishin-ryū Yamaguchi Ha Publishing Division 英信流山内派出版局, 2004.
- Gekkan Kendō Nippon Henshūbu 月刊剣道日本編集部. *Tora no Maki Sono Ichi, Ni, San and Shi* 虎の巻その壹、弍、参、四. Tokyo 東京都: Ski Journal 株式会社スキージャーナル, 2008, 2009, 2010, 2012.

Further Reading:

- Kamimoto Eiichi 紙本栄一. *Musō Shinden-ryū Iai* 夢想神伝流居合. Komae 狛江市: Ichijō Shorin 一条書林, 1985.
- Gotō Miki 後藤美基. *Iaidō no Giron- Eishin Ryū Gotō Ha Nyūmon* 居合道の理論—英信流後藤派入門. Tokyo 東京都: Kōdansha 講談社, 1979.
- Mitani Yoshisato 三谷義里. *Yōkai Iai Musō Jikiden Eishin-ryū* 詳解居合 無双直伝英信流. Tokyo 東京都: Ski Journal Co., Ltd. 株式会社スキージャーナル, 1986.
- Iwata Norikazu 岩田憲一. *Koryū Iai no Hondō Zenkai* 古流居合の本道 全解. Tokyo 東京都: Ski Journal 株式会社スキージャーナル, 2002.

BOOK MARK

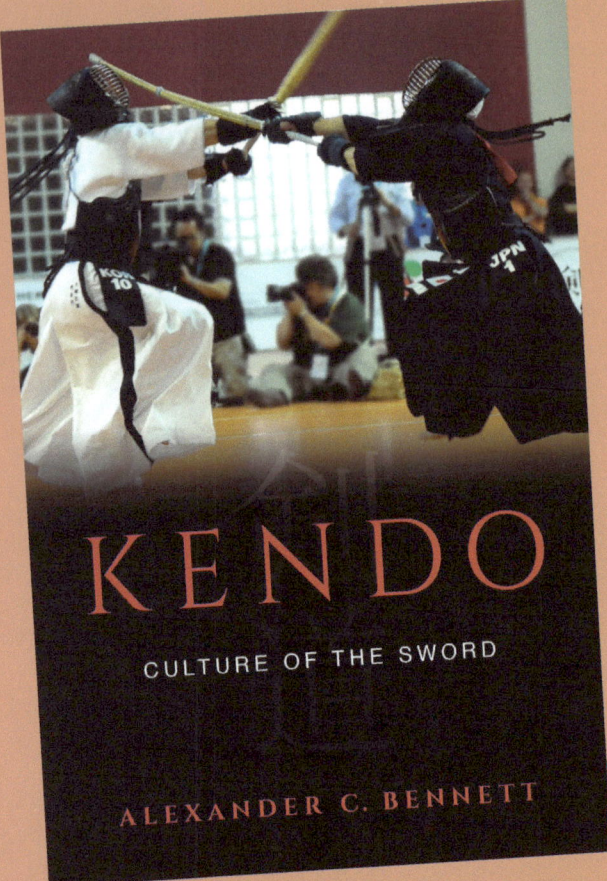

Reviewed by Antony Cundy

I openly admit, before claims of bias are leveled, that I have known the author for over twenty years. Nevertheless, I am not a modern kendo practitioner, my path having lead to the classical sword arts, and therefore was frankly not looking forward to reading a book on its present incarnation.

I am pleased to say my concerns were ill founded. This is undoubtedly the most comprehensive treatise on the evolution of the Japanese sword arts of the last 40 years and perhaps, the most important.

What we read is not the book of a fanatic, it is the labor of love from a highly respected historian and lecturer. The fact that Bennett is also a senior practitioner of the modern art of kendo makes his emic insight all the more revealing and compelling.

The book begins with an elongated prologue introducing Bennett's personal initiation into kendo, written in unmistakable 'Alex' style. Recalling his first visit to the school kendo dojo, he remarks on the sensei (Darth Vader incarnate) and the training itself. After receiving the students' attacks,

> '..Vader upped the ante, retaliating with vicious thrusts to the throat, body clashes that sent the attacker flying backward, and foot sweeps that reduced him to a sagging heap on the floor. Just when it looked as if submission were his only option, the young jedi somehow sprang to life again, and the painful process started all over. Corporal punishment had just been outlawed back in New Zealand, and thoughts that somebody should call the police crossed my mind as I stared in disbelief at the savagery.'

Witty, beautifully descriptive and immediately relatable, this is Alex at his engaging best.

Unfortunately, this is immediately followed by the driest description of the modern practice of kendo that could be imagined and I was greatly concerned that there would be no butter for the toast if this was to be the style of the whole.

However, leaving this prologue behind the Dr. Bennett of the equation smoothly guides the reader through six chapters and 237 pages, ranging from "The art of killing", an overview of the birth of classical swordsmanship, through to the global diffusion of kendo, a concerning look at the expansion of the art. All are delivered with practised ease and definitive breadth. It is exceptionally compelling reading.

There are gems of information for the budo practitioner, of all backgrounds and experiences, littering each page. For example, we learn that,

> "Kanō borrowed the idea of *dan* ranks from the grading system introduced in the board game Go during the early Tokugawa period. These modifications gave learners tangible goals to strive for, and those who passed the 1-dan rank (*shodan*) were awarded the distinction of being allowed to wear black sashes to secure their training tops."

We also learn, through the diaries of Muta Bunnosuke Takaatsu, who visited many dojo during the late 19th century and met most of the famous swordsmen in do, that the heroes of this time were not as impressive as we are led to believe. Indeed, Muta did not think much of any of them. His comments, in particular relating to Chiba Shūsaku's Genbukan, are surprisingly direct and often damning. I have never seen these quoted before in English.

I must also admit to an almost total lack of awareness of the period of kendo's evolution after the Second World War in which it was called *shinai-kyōgi*. This period seemed to the people involved at the time, as perhaps being the only way to continue in some manner their beloved sport, while living up to the new pacifistic leaning of a country badly damaged after the war. It was however, a period when kendo became for disciples an activity 'to learn about the enjoyment of sport- nothing more, and nothing less.' Thankfully, kendo evolved past this point. Furthermore, Bennett provides some succinct descriptions of obfuscated lore. In describing the founding of classical *ryūha* he states,

> "The juxtaposition of aesthetic and religious paradigms with empirical knowledge is what gave each of these schools their signature qualities."

Argue against that. Bennett also makes some biting comments in relation to the state of kobudo in Japan,

> "The number of schools represented at various kobudo demonstration events is also dwindling, and the technical quality of many of the performances is questionable."

He also gives short shrift to writers such as Noel Perrin, who he slams as being "simply wrong".

I was also pleased to see that there was no bias at work in his comprehension of the modern workings of kendo federations and the expected results of kendo practice. He writes,

> "..although I have been a devoted kendo practitioner for over two decades and truly believe in the potential kendo has for positive personal cultivation, I am enormously wary of the common attitude that one can become a "good person just by taking up kendo…"

He also gives short shrift to the Korean perversion of kendo, kumdo, which he describes as a "questionable sideshow in the development and promulgation of kendo."

It's hard to find fault in this work, and I attempted to be as harshly objective as possible, believe me I tried. There are few lapses in the otherwise comprehensive attention to detail. We are left none the wiser as to what *inu ou mono* or *kasagake* are, and I disagree that when a warrior's arrows ran out he would likely reach for his sword, spear wounds being far more common in battle.

I also believe that the description of modern kendo would have been better in the back of the book as an appendix. But let's be honest, in a book with such a monumental scope these are trifles.

However, running throughout each chapter there is a sense of fragility, concern and ambiguity. Kendo's intrinsic dichotomy, as both sporting and martial art, has become its greatest asset and, according to Bennett, its greatest dilemma. The ability to communicate and define the practice of and reason for engaging in kendo are clearly a source of much friction and Bennett's own descriptor, "spiritual sports" seems handy but uninspiring.

It is also clear that the Japanese are working hard to maintain a central control over kendo's future, so as to avoid the fate of modern judo. We can but hope that more people will follow Bennett into helping guide it away from evangelistic exclusivity toward a more structured inclusiveness.

So, in the final analysis, has the author become "complicit" in disseminating Japanese propaganda about the way of the sword as he himself fears? I believe not. Instead, Bennett has written the defining history of swordsmanship in Japan, in the English language, and helped raise these arts from esoteric fetish to cultural asset worthy of academic study at the highest level and practice by a far wider group of individuals.

Kendo: Culture of the Sword is available from the University of California Press (ISBN 978-0-520-28437-1)

Demonstrating at the Kyoto Taikai

Rene van Amersfoort: Jodo 8-dan

By Jeff Broderick

"Did you hear the news? A European passed eighth dan in jodo!"

It is an event that many people thought was years, if not decades away. But at the Kyoto Taikai in May of this year, Rene van Amersfoort, 60, of the Netherlands, beat the expectations and joined the exalted ranks of All Japan Kendo Federation (AJKF) 8-dan in jodo. Van Amersfoort's achievement is remarkable because, although there are a number of Japanese-born kendoka who have attained 8-dan while living abroad, the only other foreign-born individual to reach that rank in any AJKF budo (kendo, iaido, or jodo) is kendoka Roberto Kishikawa from Brazil. Kishikawa-sensei has long had one foot planted in Japan thanks to his Japanese heritage and language ability, in addition to a stint spent living in Japan as a graduate student. Van Amersfoort's accomplishment is another watershed moment because, not only is he a non-Japanese, but he has done all of his training, with the exception of short but regular visits to Japan, while living in Europe.

Van Amersfoort's budo career began after a ten-year stint in the Dutch Royal Navy, when he started Wado-ryū karate-do. He has since become a licensed teacher in that art and reached the level of 5-dan. In 1980 he saw a demonstration of kendo and iaido by husband-and-wife team Jolanda Dekker and Louis Vitalis of the Museido Dojo in Amsterdam. This event changed his life: fascinated by what he saw, Van Amersfoort began training in both arts and soon added jodo to his busy schedule. As if four arts were somehow insufficient, he also trained in kickboxing. Whoever said, "If you chase two rabbits you won't catch either of them," obviously never met Rene van Amersfoort.

In 1984, he established the Kiryoku Dojo in his home city of Zoetermeer, near The Hague, where he began by teaching karate, adding jodo and iaido a few years later.

Through his ongoing training with Vitalis-sensei, he became connected with Edo Kōkichi-sensei, Iijima-sensei, and Ishidō Shizufumi-sensei of the Shinbukan dojo, becoming a student in the lineage of the late Hiroi-sensei. After starting to teach jodo in 1986, and iaido in 1992, Van Amersfoort took on teaching duties for the Dutch national iaido and jodo teams for the European Championships while Vitalis-sensei was living in Japan. From 1996, after reaching 5-dan in both iaido and jodo, he began teaching internationally. In 1998, together with his teacher Vitalis, he went to Osaka where they challenged 6-dan jodo; both passed. They went again in January 2005, this time to Tokyo to challenge their 7-dan. Again, both passed.

Van Amersfoort credits this success to three days of intensive training with Ishidō- and Yano-sensei at Ishidō's Kawasaki dojo, "something we will never forget". Over the years at various European jodo seminars and tournaments, he has been fortunate to meet and train under a veritable who's who of top Japanese jodo sensei: Hiroi Tsunetsugu, Namitome Shigenori, Yano Shoichirō, Ishidō Shizufumi, Shiiya Mitsuo, Ōtake Toshiyuki, Nishiumi Kamatarō, Shōji Keiichi, and more. He also met Yoshimura Ken'ichi at many jodo and iaido seminars, and through the experience of shared practice, the two became good friends. For the past five years, they have performed jodo *embu* at the Kyoto Taikai together. But of them all, he still considers Louis Vitalis to be his direct mentor.

Vam Amersfoort, back left, at the Museido Dojo. Front row (l-r), Jolanda Dekker, Louis Vitalis-sensei, Ishidō-sensei

"It was Vitalis Sensei who, as a teacher and as a person, motivated me to develop and deepen my studies of iaido and jodo, and nowadays, to practise kendo again," he says. By 1992, Van Amersfoort had given up practising kendo, but on Vitalis' urging, he has once more added it to his practice and teaching schedule. He is currently 3-dan in kendo, and is looking forward to challenging 4-dan in August of this year at the summer seminar in Amsterdam. The two remain very active, together taking care of technical support and training for the Dutch jodo team.

His recent 8-dan success came on only his second attempt, something that few can boast of. In his first attempt, in May of 2015, he reached the second of two rounds of testing, becoming the first non-Japanese ever to do so. But he ultimately fell short. He reflects: "Last year in 2015 I was too compact, and in some techniques I had problems doing the Seitei-gata with opponents who were smaller than myself. Also, my movements needed to be more relaxed, smoother, and bigger. For example, I was told that my exam last year was a good *embu,* but my thinking and my execution were too square. It needed to be more rounded, as in more spontaneous." He set about changing his techniques, making them softer, smoother, and more technically correct.

"With the help of Hayashi Eiko-sensei–we trained in Ishidō-sensei's dojo in Kawasaki–I was pushed to sharpen my sword side and change my *jō* techniques in several places." His efforts came to fruition this year. "It was of course an exciting moment!" he recalls.

Now, his name goes down in jodo history, but he hasn't let that go to his head.

"I'm realising that I'm still a beginner in jodo. Now it starts. Deeper training–more effective and efficient training–has to follow." But in the end, it still comes down to basics: "*Keiko, keiko, keiko,* and *benkyō, benkyō, benkyō* [study]."

What advice does Van Amersfoort-sensei have for jodoka around the world? "Devotion and determination to follow your sensei without any doubts is necessary to develop to a higher level. Copy what your sensei is doing, and preserve what you have learned to reach higher technically. Try to bring your image and your reality closer together. *Gambatte kudasai*! [Please try your best!]"

Bujutsu Jargon Part 9

Reference guide covering various bujutsu-related terminology

Bruce Flanagan MA
Lecturer - Kaichi International University

59 兵法 *heihō*

Methods of traditional combat and warfare including individual combat and large-scale battlefield strategy. Another reading of the term is *hyōhō*. The term was also used interchangeably to refer to *bujutsu* or weapons systems such as *kenjutsu*. A warrior could be called a *hyōhō-sha* (兵法者). A strategist or tactician could be called a *heihō-ka* (兵法家) or *heihōgaku-sha* (兵法学者). A military text is called a *heihō-sho* (兵法書). *Heihō* can also be called *heigaku* (兵学).

60 軍学 *gungaku*

Military science or the study of warfare. Can also be called *gunjigaku* (軍事学) or *gunpō* (軍法). Included overall campaign strategy (*sakusen-keikaku* 作戦計画), troop placements (*yōhei* 用兵), and combat tactics (*senjutsu* 戦術), while often utilising meteorology, astronomy, and divination. Early strategies were heavily influenced by Chinese military texts and many schools existed including the Kōshū-ryū, Echigo-ryū, Hōjō-ryū, Yamaga-ryū, Naganuma-ryū, and Kusunoki-ryū. A military scientist or scholar was called a *gungaku-sha* (軍学者).

61 上座 *kamiza*

Traditionally the seats in a room or the space in a dojo reserved for important guests, instructors, judges or referees. The *kamiza* might be a *tokonoma*-style alcove or elevated area decorated with calligraphy, flags, flowers, or pictures, and may be floored with *tatami* mats. The instructor is generally positioned close to the *kamiza* while the practising students are closer to the 'rear' or 'less important' area of the dojo known as the *shimoza* (下座). In a smaller dojo, the *kamiza* might constitute an entire interior wall which may not necessarily be the *shōmen* or 'front' wall of the dojo. Related terms: *jōseki* (上席), *shimoseki* (下席).

62 神棚 *kamidana*

Small decorative Shinto altars found in homes and businesses and often in martial arts dojo. They are generally placed on a shelf, or a rack is mounted onto a wall if space is limited. Often constructed as small replicas of Shinto shrines, *kamidana* contain various protective charms and symbolic items to ward off misfortune or disaster.

 # 63 活人剣 katsujin-ken

A sword is a lethal weapon but the manner is which a sword is used is determined by the nature and intentions of the person wielding it. If a sword is wielded with 'good' intentions such as to protect or defend, then this state is described as the 'life-giving sword' (*katsujin-ken*). The sword may also be used for a noble purpose such as cultivating the mind of the swordsman through martial training. This concept was described by Yagyū Munenori in *Heihō Kadensho* (兵法家伝書), his famous text on strategy and swordsmanship. In contrast, he descibed the 'life-taking sword' wielded with murderous intent as *satsujin-ken* (殺人剣) or *setsunin-tō* (殺人刀).

 # 64 居合 iai

Quickly drawing one's sword from its scabbard and cutting one's opponent down on the spot in order to swiftly end the encounter without extended swordplay. The first character, *i* (居), means 'on the spot', and the second character, *ai* (合), refers to drawing and cutting at close-range. Drawing the sword is called *battō* (抜刀) or *bakken* (抜剣) and these specialised drawing and cutting techniques came to be known as *iaijutsu* and *battō-jutsu*. Drawing and cutting in *iai*-style was also known as *iai-nuki* (居合抜き) and the skill was historically used in crowd-drawing street performances by sales merchants. Many different schools of *iaijutsu* still exist and some have now been stylised into the modern martial art form of iaido (居合道). Focus is also placed on shaking blood off the blade (*chiburi* 血振り) and returning the sword to its scabbard (*nōtō* 納刀). Iaido techniques can be performed from standing or seated positions such as *seiza* and *tatehiza*. Crouching down while one's hips and one knee is raised in preparation to draw and cut is known as *iai-goshi* (居合腰).

 # 65 陰陽 on-yō

China's *yin* and *yang* philosophy was imported to Japan, and it was pronounced *in* and *yō*. The field or practice of divination is known as *ekigaku* (易学). Divination based on *in* and *yō* and the *five elements* (*gogyō* 五行) wood, fire, earth, metal, and water, such as *feng shui* (*fūsui* 風水), was practised widely in Japan. The localised practice came to be pronounced *onyō* or *onmyō*, the divination art itself became known as *onyō-dō* (陰陽道). An authorized practitioner was called an *onyō-ji* (陰陽師).

Bibliography

- *Nihon Budō Jiten* (*Zusetsu*), Sasama Y., Kashiwa-Shobō, 2003.
- *Kōjien* (*Daigohan*), Iwanami Shoten, 2004.

鎧兜
A GUIDE TO JAPANESE ARMOUR

Text and Photos: Jo Anseeuw – Association for the Research and Preservation of Japanese Helmets and Armour

This fabulous *kabuto* from the collection of Luc Taelman (Belgium) was made by one of the main armour makers of the Saotome school, Saotome Iechika.

The Saotome school was a prominent school of armour production in Japan, alongside other schools such as Myōchin, Haruta, Iwai, Nagasone, and Bamen. Traditionally, the roots of the Saotome school are dated to around the Tenbun period (1532–1555), an assumption based on one 52-plate *kabuto* with a signature that has been dated to 1569. Research into these *kabuto* is difficult, not only because of the lack of other dated pieces, but also because there are many fake genealogies from the Edo period (1603–1868). Furthermore, as is often the case, many new writers simply copy old information without conducting extra research themselves.

- **Name of Piece:**
Tetsu sabiji 8 ken so fukurin shiinari kabuto
(鉄錆地六間総覆輪椎形兜)

- **Craftsman:**
Jōshū-jū Saotome Iechika
(常州住早乙女家親)

Over the last 25 years, Teruo Orikasa, a Japanese armour researcher, has examined over 200 Saotome helmets from all over Japan. He is confident that the signature on the *kabuto* on which the start date of the Saotome school is based, is actually a later attribution. According to his research, the origin of the Saotome school is probably situated around the Keichō period (1596–1615), or maybe even somewhat later. Consequently, this means that most Saotome *kabuto*, although considered the ultimate in helmet construction and elegance, have probably never seen war.

Saotome Iechika lived during the early to mid Edo period, in Hitachi province, and is considered to be one of the early grandmasters of the school. As is the case, however, with many other armour smiths, differences in workmanship and signature styles indicate that there were probably at least three craftsmen with the same name who were active during that period. Therefore, an exact date of when he worked is impossible to state. Some old documents, however, indicate Iechika as being of the 5th generation of the Saotome school, but the school's official documents were destroyed at the end of the Edo period.

Iechika made several *shiinari* (acorn) shaped *kabuto*. This particular eight-plate *kabuto*, made in *tetsu sabiji* (russet iron), has a very high degree of finishing and the custom-made leaf motive decorations indicate that it was probably made for a *daimyō* of the Abe clan, information that is also written on the *bitsu*. The *wakidate* (side decoration) is a realistic lacquered reproduction of deer antlers, which symbolise the messengers of the gods. This tradition had already started on very early *kabuto*, in the form of *kuwagata*. These *kuwagata* were mounted on the front of the *kabuto* and were flat pieces of metal that were shaped to represent deer antlers.

For more information about Japanese armour, please see my website: www.katchu-no-bi.com

鎧 兜 A GUIDE TO JAPANESE ARMOUR

SHOGUN KENDOGU
by kazutaka 一貴

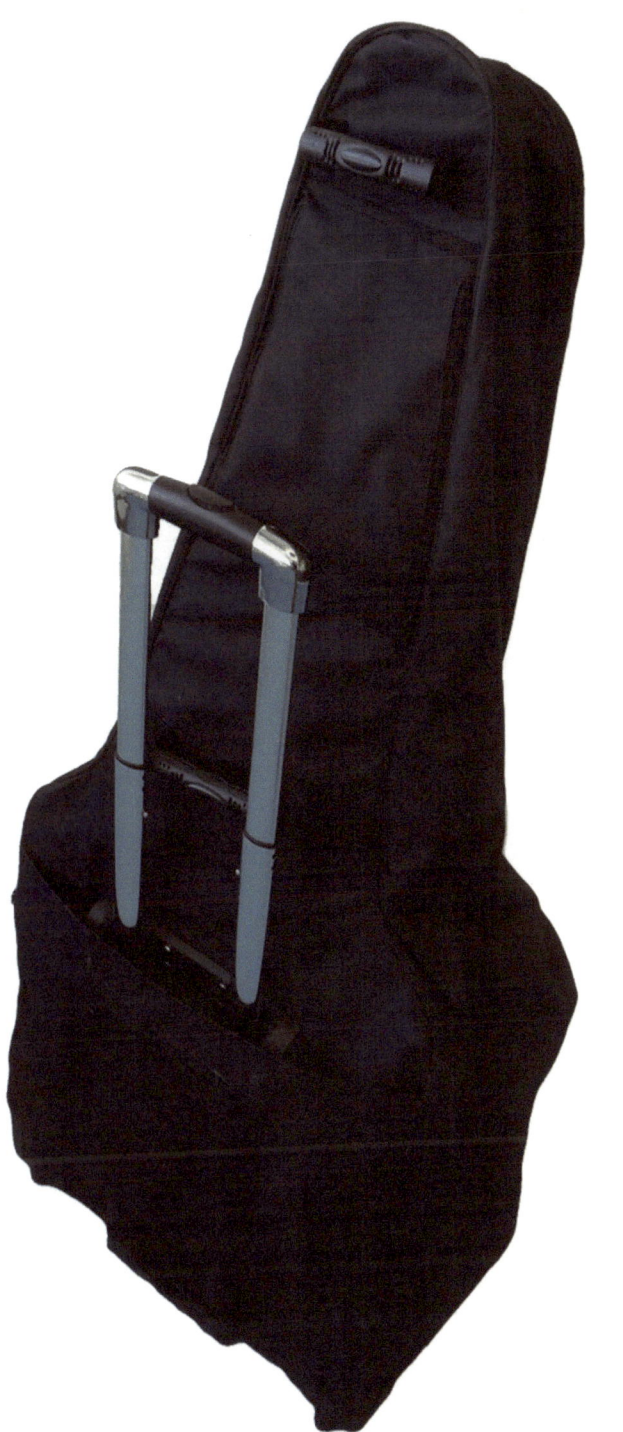

First of its kind, seasoned kendo traveller **Alex Bennett** has teamed up with Shogun Kendogu to create the Shogun Traveller Bag™.

Allowing you to combine your shinai with your other luggage, you can now travel abroad and minimise extra luggage costs charged by many airlines.

If your airline charges extra to check-in more than one item, simply insert your shinai inside the Shogun Traveller Bag™. If your airline charges more for over-sized baggage, simply roll it down and check your shinai in separately as usual.

Big enough to pack clothes, dōgi, bōgu, and 3 shinai, the Shogun Traveller Bag™ is made with durable yet light weight material.

We have kept the extras to a minimum to ensure the overall weight of your one-piece check-in luggage can be packed with all the necessities and not exceed the specified weight.

RRP US$249
(international shipping included)

The *original* Shogun Traveller Bag™
a new way for kendoists to travel

> **shugyō** (n.)
> The process of rigorously training and polishing one's mind and body. See *musha-shugyō*.
>
> (AJKF, *Japanese-English Dictionary of Kendo*)

The Shugyō Mind: Part 2   By Alex Bennett

"Training because you 'want to', and training because you 'have to' are completely different in quality and meaning..."

We have all been there. A cold rainy night, interesting stuff on the TV, a strong feeling of apathy justified in your mind by the intolerable stress you've been subjected to during the day. And, you have a pain in your foot/finger/butt. It's better to take training off tonight and let yourself recover from your current state of fatigue. Besides, there is no point in going to training if you can't do your best, right? It would be "rude" to your training partners… That's how you convince yourself that it would benefit nobody if you reluctantly went to the dojo under such dire circumstances.

Sometimes you stay home having successfully persuaded yourself that you are right, but you still have to subdue the odd pangs of guilt that emerge from within because you actually know who you are kidding. Or, you may say to yourself "No! Get hard. I HAVE to go to training if I want to get good. And, what would my sensei/peers think if I didn't go?" So, you go. Not entirely happy about the prospect of undergoing a demanding training session that day, you are a slave to your guilt and desire to do the "right thing". By the night's end you are glad you went, and sheepishly, albeit privately, lament the energy you wasted arguing the pros and cons with yourself beforehand.

This happens occasionally to all of us. We are, after all, only human. If it is a regular torment, then you would be well advised to think long and hard about whether kendo is something that you honestly want to do. We are adults, and we are allowed to make our own minds up. What about children though? Kids often don't have a choice. All dojos have a mixture of children who genuinely want to be there, and those who are made to go by their parents who see kendo as an essential part of their education. At least, that is the case in Japan.

Even if the child is gifted with sublime natural ability, and shines above all others in the *shiai-jō*, his or her days in the dojo are probably numbered if they are there simply because s/he has to be. They will keep going for as long as mum and dad make them, and may enjoy success in competitions and revel in the attention, but ultimately they are just surfing a temporary wave, and will jump off to seek other thrills when they find their true passion. If the kid is blessed with an inspiring instructor, then the passion can be nurtured. For this reason, the burden of teaching is truly immense, but that is another article…

On the other hand, there are kids who have an insatiable passion for kendo, but try as they may, they never manage to excel. S/he may be hopelessly uncoordinated and lack the cheeky nous required to bring home trophies. But, it doesn't matter to them. They just love turning up and throwing themselves into the melee. If training is early morning on the weekends, they will be up at the crack of dawn ready to go, leaving sleep deprived mums and dads in a state of ambivalence.

Indeed, the typical dojo is a polarised mix of passion, motivation, and skill. One of the beautiful aspects of kendo, however, is that it's a world in which the tortoise always prevails in the end. The rabbit might be dexterous and swift, but it is the plodding tortoise that makes it to the finish line first. Of course, there is no finish line in kendo, but effort and years in the dojo is the great equaliser. Irrespective of whether you start kendo as a tot or in midlife, ultimately it is the passion rather than inherent skill that drives one to the summit. What is passion? It is a mindset.

In this sense, whether or not you have the drive to traverse the perpetual path of kendo is plainly evident in the pre-training internal conversation with yourself. Do you really want to improve of your own volition, or do you struggle to convince yourself that you 'should' make the effort? Put another way, are going to training because you "want to", or because you feel that you "have to"? No matter how strong your dojo is, or how famous your sensei may be, if you are not there for anything other than your own passionate dictate, you will never fulfil your true potential. Knowing, or at least accepting why you subject yourself to the rigours and odours of kendo is perhaps one of the toughest battles you will face, and it is always up and down.

So, what do you do? Being "convinced of your passion" as you traipse down the hard road is never easy. You will waiver, and will be tempted by the easy route, or the exit sign. You might sense the romance of kendo, but you will also come to doubt if it has any true meaning to your life and existence. That is the toughest test of all. It's easy to give up because it's impossible to really know the value of an unbroken constant that links all the stages of your life. I'm not there either, but I trust my sensei who are in their eighties and nineties when they tell me, "It was absolutely worth it. You won't know until you near the end, but make sure you pursue something throughout your life."

Back to present reality though, if you can somehow train your mind to relish the task ahead rather than nit-pick the pros and cons—in other words, learn how to flick the switch into "just get hard and do mode" rather than "debate mode"—you might find your passion grow in spite of itself. I remember an epiphany I had a few years back regarding mindset. It was during the gruelling two-week mid-winter training at a formidable kendo university in Osaka. Trainings started at 5:30am. Getting out of my warm bed in the dorm to walk three minutes to the dojo in the freezing cold, ready to start a three-hour marathon of *kirikaeshi*, *kakari-geiko*, and general nastiness was… well let's just say somewhat depressing. It took all of my internal strength and then some to put on the wet *gi* and walk the green mile into the fray.

Then an interesting thing happened. Being two weeks long, each day had its own trials and tribulations. Call it biorhythm, or just the vicissitudes of daily life, but in spite of the discomfort some mornings I would feel on top of the world as I took that three-minute walk. "Bring it on!" I would say to myself. Then, other mornings I would be filled with dread. Guess which days turned out to be the great ones. Success or failure, pleasure or pain, love or loss was all decided in the three-minute walk from the mundane to the insane. I learned that if you are going to do something, you might as well do it single-mindedly with a positive attitude, even if that means feigning it sometimes. Yes, it works when you feign it, too! But it's a skill that takes developing until it becomes habitual. It becomes a part of you that you can't do without, and the mindset is transferable to many other aspects of your life. Nobody said it was meant to be easy, but that's *shugyō* for you.

The Rokudan Road

By Sue Lytollis

This is an article on how I, a female kenshi, tried to pass 6-dan from the age of 49 to 55. I was finally successful, but anyone who is desperately climbing that *dan* ladder might find what I have written below to be of some use.

What did I learn?

Well, after acquiring 5-dan, one waits another five years before being eligible for 6-dan. Trying for 6-dan from a country with no resident 7-dan (pleased to say that we do now!) and teaching at a small dojo with approximately 15 members, is a psychological challenge. We do not have the luxury of training five times a week under austere 7-or 8-dan sensei like those living in Japan.

Typically, most 5-dan kenshi teach several times a week, for free, to a bunch of very committed and lovely kendoka in their little town. They would also most likely be the highest grade member in their club, with little challenge except the odd hard hit from a beginner, or a sneaky manoeuvre from one of the young *dan* holders. They may still well be paying off the expenses of their last round of out of town refereeing, or being on a grading panel in some far-flung part of the country. They are well meaning, and may make time to read *Kendo World* and the latest books giving advice on how to pass grades. What I learnt is that all of this is important, but trying for 6-dan in particular is a very personal journey.

After the joy of passing 5-dan, the intensity of training and the wonder of having this senior grade wears in, and before you know it, you are ready to line up against new 6-dans to see what kind of "magic" their kendo has inspired. So what is it that you need to do to push yourself out of the 5-dan zone and edge yourself closer to the next goal? What can possibly change in your fine execution of *men*, *kote*, and *dō*, and your fabulous *ōji-waza*?

If you are, like me, one of the kendo pioneers in a small country, then you may very well be in your 50s – not exactly in the prime of your life! The additional challenges are managing that middle-age spread, fighting off those hungry 3-dan, and pitching your sensei-self as a good role model. You may be doing this by yourself, with no-one higher to reflect upon your kendo with. So, after all those years of kendo, you are thinking, "I must change something in my *waza* to impress the examiners in the next expensive trip to Japan (or other region) so that I can achieve the next grade!" Time flies by and before you know it you are "in season" to try for 6-dan.

If you are in a good kendo scene, you may have other 5-, 6- or even 7-dan sensei in your country encouraging you along. It is important for these kendo folk to support you and commiserate with you. Like you, they have likely tried and failed, but have also gone on to greater things. Do not be shy about asking them for their personal wisdom and support in your journey.

In my journey to pass 6-dan I have:

1 — Read Yoshiyama Mitsuru-sensei's fabulous book on grading, took notes and re-read them prior to grading.
2 — Attended some amazing *gasshuku* from the likes of Mochizuki-sensei, Morioka-sensei, Inoue-sensei (long time visitors to NZ), etc. and took copious notes and reflected with meaning on what they have said.
3 — Asked my peers esoteric questions and had esoteric responses, e.g. "What do you need to do to pass?" – "Hell I don't know, but I did in the end!"; or, "It's all very Zen at that level."
4 — Attended two Gedatsukai Summer Seminars where I took the grading, but failed, and also at Novarra where I failed, too. My guess is that representing NZ at *shiai* and then heading into a 6-dan grading was just too much to make an appropriate change.
5 — Prayed at innumerable shrines and temples, and bought various *omamori* (talismans)
6 — Received creative visualisation training from a senior workmate.
7 — Been to the gym. Lost 24 kilos; put on another 10.
8 — Stopped drinking; drunk too much.
9 — Took up box fit and gym work.
10— Seen students begin kendo and reach their 3-dan, all while I thrash away at 6-dan!

So what flipped for me in 2015 to be successful? For the sake of helping others, in this article I'd like to share some insights.

I had a goal

As I was going to the Nippon Budokan for the 16th WKC as an NZ coach, I decided to take the grading there. I think that fighting against other non-Japanese is better for me than a regular Japanese 6-dan grading where I would be pitched against men in their mid-50s—the pinnacle of their training—who have 8-dan guiding them along their way. I would much rather be up against people in a similar situation to myself, those with their little dojo and who are lucky if they can train more than three or four times a week. In February, I asked for the help of NZ's most recently graded 6-dan, Lee-sensei, and established the best night to train with him.

I had a frustrating lesson with Lee-sensei where my every move was nit-picked and disassembled. I was told, in no uncertain terms, "You must not flinch, you must not show doubt, you must be able to 'know' or create a time for your opponent to attack, and you must take advantage of that. You must do beautiful kendo and you must make them afraid of you. You must dominate, dominate, dominate, exterminate!" I used various *seme men* exercises to work on a short, snappy *men* that would result in getting the *shodachi men* strike, if all went well. For a time, I became obsessed with trying to get the first *men* in every fight I attempted with anyone. I even tried to beat people onto the bus in my determination to "be first"!

To get ready, I also tried to find "old men" my age to train with. A local Japanese 5-dan, Masaki, was a blessing, even though I am at least 10 years his

At the WKC in Tokyo

senior. I also practised with Liz, my 5-dan peer, to do mock gradings as well. My reasoning was that I was more likely, in a grading for non-Japanese, to come up against male opponents. I also filmed my one-minute mock *shinsa* trainings and (over) critiqued my performances.

One breakthrough occurred when I was fighting Masaki. He was fighting quite close, I said, "Can you move back mate? My opponents won't do that in the grading." He replied, "Well if your *seme* was stronger, I wouldn't be able to get in that close!" Eye opening. I then focused on the perennial problem I knew I had which was my *kensen* being too high. I lowered my *chūdan* appropriately, focused, and began to keep Masaki at bay. I also learnt from various opponents small but simple ways to begin to sense when they were preparing to strike. I practised forcing myself into their space and striking with a sharp and tight *men*, or reacting appropriately with *kaeshi-dō*, *de-gote*, *debana-men*, etc. It was like turning on a switch and seeing kendo anew.

In addition to *keiko*, I also sought guidance from a sports hypnotherapist; something I found beneficial. He told me that regarding success or failure, the biggest opponent is yourself; your fears, doubts, insecurities, disbelief in your abilities. This together with thinking that your opponent is better, faster, thinner, better looking, more experienced, better instructed, a monster in armour, etc. All of this is all in your own head. I couldn't blame anyone else!

Andrew Hardwick, my hypnotherapist who I absolutely recommend and who works by Skype, took me on a little *shiai* in my head with myself. You will be pleased to know that ultimately I won. It was a good feeling, and from then on progress was palpable. Experiencing these techniques first hand was worth every penny. When you think that the average cost of attending a 6-dan grading in Japan from New Zealand is at least $5000, then a few hundred dollars on a mind magician is well worth the value.

In the following weeks I learnt ways to relax, manage flagging energy, turn up the volume on my emotions of pride, calm, power, beauty and attack. On the way, I learnt that I can help myself sleep, warm up my feet, cool down when the Japanese summer has a heatwave, and even make my posture stronger. My confidence grew, and my grim determination to survive the three weeks prior to my grading intensified.

I was part of the NZ team preparing for the World Kendo Championships. While trying to support the team (and coach my one female kenshi) I had to juggle my own needs and a desire not to get an injury. Having Bennett-sensei (NZ Team Coach) in the dojo also helped. One comment he gave me really helped. "You only need one good *men* and a good *debana-kote* to pass." He said. This gave me confidence. It broke down my fear of *having* to get the *shodachi men* and put me into thinking, OK—I get two one-minute fights, I do not have to score too many points, it is quality not quantity. He gave me some exercises where, with his *seme*, he would make a move and I was to catch his *kote* or *men* without faltering. This was good. On my quest to find "old men" to train with, I went to my old buddies at Amagasaki Kendo Club and found their unfailing support and belief in me very encouraging.

I put several things on the wall of my hotel room. I made myself a mock 6-dan grading certificate signed by "five very impressed 8-dan", and I also had a large page on which I wrote all the bits of advice I had been given in the preceding week: Stare them in the eyes, make them afraid of you. Do beautiful kendo. Relax your arms after the *men* cut. Do your own kendo.

I made a little makeshift shrine in my room with a lovely Daruma given to me by a friend. I thought of the many great sensei that had passed in recent years, all of whom would be up there supporting me: Ron Bennett (Australia), Terry Holt (UK), Inoue Yoshihiko (Shizuoka), and from a long time ago, Suzuki-sensei from Kodokan dojo in Kyoto; they were all there, together with the hopes and dreams of my partner and my club, Yoshinkan.

But before my big day on June 1, 2015, I had three days of kendo to endure. I was supporting the Kiwi team, watching some awesome competitors from around the world, and exploring the many levels of the Nippon Budokan to meet friends from around the world. For a 55-year-old, it was very tiring.

Before I knew it, I was at the Sayonara party and had one glass of wine. In my previous attempts I had a strict "no alcohol the night before" rule. This time, though, I thought, "What the hell, I may as well so long as I don't get bladdered!" I was able to relax. Still, I made it to bed at 11.30pm and slept like a log. By the day of the grading, I had well and truly used my mind management skills learnt in my sports hypnotherapy classes to lay waste to any silly thoughts I had about: a) coming up against opponents with really weird kendo; b) not being able to zing; c) getting creamed in my first fight. I was quietly determined to perform my best *waza*.

I stood in the hall at the Olympic Centre with the sense that I was on another planet. My two male opponents were in front of me, and both were on the short side. I was able to watch them fight and then take on the first one.

I cannot give a detailed description of my grading, but I felt good especially after my first fight and I felt that I had achieved two of those important cuts that Bennett-sensei had mentioned. As I walked off the court after my second fight, Bennett-sensei gave me the "glad eye", so I was hopeful. When the results came out I was shocked; my number was not on the top row of numbers of successful 6-dan candidates, and I thought I had not passed! However, as I was the oldest examinee in my group, my number had snuck down to the second line. Until someone confirmed that my number was there, my jubilation was not fully released. Phew!

Now comes that spectacular time when you "think" you have passed, but you still have 10 minutes of *kata* to go. I found my partner's *kata* somewhat weak. However, I channelled my love and appreciation of Inoue-sensei's great teaching into my *kata* and felt that I had done my best. All of us that did the *kata* were herded into a group and told that we all passed. It was a historic day for me, and also for NZ kendo with young Blake passing 6-dan at the age of 32, and Graham Sayer finally passing 7-dan after many attempts. Our only sadness was that Alan Stephenson was unsuccessful in his 7-dan *shinsa*.

How can I describe what it is like to be a 6-dan, a female 6-dan, and the first one for New Zealand? It is a feeling that the 35 years spent training has been worthwhile, and that it is time to celebrate and to get drunk, very drunk. 6-dan is another step in your kendo career as you can now help grade to 4-dan in your small country and you can continue to be a role model for women and all people who will step into your dojo in their baggie pants and hopeful eyes saying, "I want to study kendo."

You aren't God—your s*@t still stinks—but by gosh do you feel damn happy!

Kendo Teachings

By Hanshi 8-dan Iwadate Saburō
Translated by Seiya Takubo

The following instructional points were collated by Hanshi 8-dan Iwadate Saburō from lessons given by Takano Sasaburō-sensei, and other associated sensei, at the Shūdōgakuin Takano Dōjō between 1936 and 1941. This information then formed the basis of a lecture given by Iwadate-sensei in October 2015 at the Shūdōkai kendo club in Inage City, Chiba prefecture.

Points to be aware of in a *dan* examination

A. *Chakusō* (proper attire): Wearing the *men*, the length of the *men-himo* (*men* cords), collar of the *keikogi* and the back, wearing the *hakama*, position of the *dō*.

B. Etiquette: *Taitō, sagetō,* where to look (*metsuke*), bows to 15° and 30° (*rei*), the spirit (*ki*) of etiquette.

C. *Sonkyo*: Holding your head straight, have strength in the knees, open up the legs and knees.

D. Posture: How to hold your *shinai, kamae, metsuke*, the position of your left foot and fist.

E. *Kihaku* (vigour): *Seme* (pressure), *zettaitekisen* (the feeling of absolute control over the line), kendo that prevents the first strike, same with the second and third strikes.

F. Attack and Defence: *Sen no waza, sensen no waza* (anticipatory techniques), movements, distance.

G. Variety of Techniques: *Sen no men, degashira-men, de-gote, nuki-dō* (techniques that are accepted as proper strikes).

H. *Zanshin*: Continued physical and mental alertness after making a strike.

Points for instruction

1. According to Shigeyoshi-sensei, as soon as many kendoka stand up, they start to move inward and shift toward the right, but this is a terrible mistake. You must have the feeling of pressuring your opponent. Even if it's only moving your big toe, you must always feel like pushing forward.

2. When doing *taiatari*, it is important to push your opponent's arms upward.

3. Some people strike their opponent's *men* while moving back (*hiki-waza*), and then immediately raise their arms over their head in the *banzai* position. This is wrong. After striking, return to *chūdan-no-kamae* and show *zanshin*.

4. After striking your opponent's right *dō*, make sure you display *zanshin* and keep watching your opponent.

5. During a grading, it is essential to have the correct attitude and posture as these will have a bearing on the final outcome. Winning is not everything.

6. As a beginner, all of your strikes and techniques should be large. Train for short periods, but with maximum effort. After you've improved to a certain level, you should then experiment with the movement of your feet.

7. The sort of *keiko* I dislike the most is when practitioners strike unnecessarily when too close to their opponent. The *shinai* should cross at about 1 *sun* (3 cm), as if the *kensaki* are stuck together with glue. If the opponent moves one step forward, take one back. If the opponent moves back, move forward. Use this to either initiate *seme* or strike the opponent.

8. In kendo, good posture is essential; bad posture is simply not kendo. As noted above, disregarding the *maai* and unnecessarily striking when too close is not good form. The moment when the *kensaki* meet, you should measure your breath, and anticipate the right instant to strike. This is when kendo is most interesting.

9. Training is not just about *you* getting better; it is for mutual improvement. If you make a mistake, it is an opportunity for your opponent to execute a technique and improve.

10. Fearing the opponent's *tsuki* will cause you to step back and continue moving back until you're lying in a heap on the floor. Therefore, if your opponent attempts to do *tsuki*, move forward. They will be unable to perform *tsuki* if the *maai* is too close. If the opponent moves back, press forward. Beginners should not strike *tsuki* or *dō*. Instead, they should focus on learning to strike *kote* and *men*. Then, *tsuki* and *dō* will come naturally.

11. When a *tsuki* is aimed through either the left or right of the enemy's *tsubamoto* (the area around the *tsuba*), or at the centreline of the opponent's *dō*, your hands will tighten. This will naturally raise the *kensen* to perform *tsuki*.

12. According to Takizawa-sensei, no one should get hurt from a *tsuki* if done with the correct feeling.

13. As stated by Kōno Hiromasa-sensei, when both kendoka are standing in *chūdan* with *kensaki* crossed and are looking to find an opportunity to strike, the only moment you can attack is at the instant one's opponent starts to attack (*debana*), or when falling back after severing the *maai*; striking at the instant the opponent moves is a good opportunity.

14. Takano Sasaburo-sensei points out mistakes in *kirikaeshi*. Sensei claims that in order to help release the excess power around your shoulders in *kirikaeshi*, you must relax and lower your shoulders, and raise both hands over your head. When striking, if you can see the *motodachi* through both arms, then it's fine; there is no need to bring your *kensen* to the point where it touches your spine. Strike as if you were to split the enemy's head in two! The vicinity of the "black dot" (the third bar on the *mengane*) should be struck diagonally from above. Do

not swing the *shinai* around horizontally. The most important thing is to make sure you bring your arms up to the point where you can see the *motodachi*. When receiving, try to bring out the opponent's strength. Therefore, try to receive as if you were absorbing the strike (*nayasu*), rather than directing it upwards, or deflecting it. Move back enough to make the opponent extend fully so that they are striking from the correct distance and with the sword's *monouchi*. [A note dated January 21, 1938]

15. It is a mistake to think that increasing the duration of *keiko* is good. Always visualise having a duel with real swords. When struck on the head, you're dead; when struck on the *kote*, you have lost an arm. Make it a three-point match; it should last two or three minutes, and should be fought with all of your might.

16. If your *kensen* is wobbling, it's due to the grip of your left hand being loose. If you tighten the left grip, your sword should not quiver. When both you and your opponent are in *chūdan* and there seems to be no opening, bring down your *kensen* and apply *seme* toward the opponent's right fist and strike as soon as they flinch. Applying *seme* and then striking will allow the opponent to recover immediately and defend. Thus, *seme* and striking should be done simultaneously.

17. People who are short in stature should stretch their body thoroughly and try to imagine looking down at the enemy's back from above.

18. Everyone seems to have a bad habit with their left wrist; you mustn't grip it with the palms upward and the thumb pointing at the opposite shoulder. The grip must be made with bent wrists and the thumbs pointing downward. By doing this you should gain some power in the *kensaki*. Then put power in the hips, correct your posture and assume *kamae*. If it comes down to *tsuba-zeriai*, receive it with your core by sticking out your stomach. Do not pull in your chin or hunch forward. This will lead to a delay in being able to strike.

19. Takano-sensei stated that a natural posture (*shizentai*) must be the basis of movement in kendo. In any strike, thrust, and movement forward or back, this natural posture must be sustained. It is said to be like the posture when walking on the road with your right leg out; in the *chūdan* stance, both hands grip the *shinai* like wringing a rag. The left hand should grip as if you were wringing out your *tenugui*, while the right hand cradles it lightly. Do not apply strength; it is said "*Ichigan-nisoku-santan-shiriki*" (first eyes, second feet, third guts, fourth technique [for a fuller explanation of this teaching, see the article "Inishie wo Kangaeru" in *Kendo World* 8.1]). It is vital to know where to fix your gaze; your eyes should gaze upon your opponent completely.

20. There are two kinds of vision, *ken* and *kan*. *Ken* is looking with your eyes; *kan* is looking with your heart. Since there can be many mistakes made using *ken* alone, do not rely on it. On the other hand, *kan* should be used more to foresee the opponent's movements. This is often effective when used in the real world. *Kanken* (*kan* and *ken* together) is very useful for prevailing in kendo as well. [A note dated July 25, 1940]

21. When exhausted, do not breathe through your mouth as this leads to the release of energy that was stored in the abdomen. Always keep your mouth shut, and constantly breathe through your nostrils.

Hanshi 8-dan Iwadate Saburō-sensei was born in Chiba prefecture in 1939. He was formerly a member of the Chiba police force's riot squad (tokuren), and subsequently became the Chiba police kendo instructor. He is the head of Shofūkan dojo and is the president of the All Japan Seniors Association. He also has extensive teaching experience in Japan and overseas.

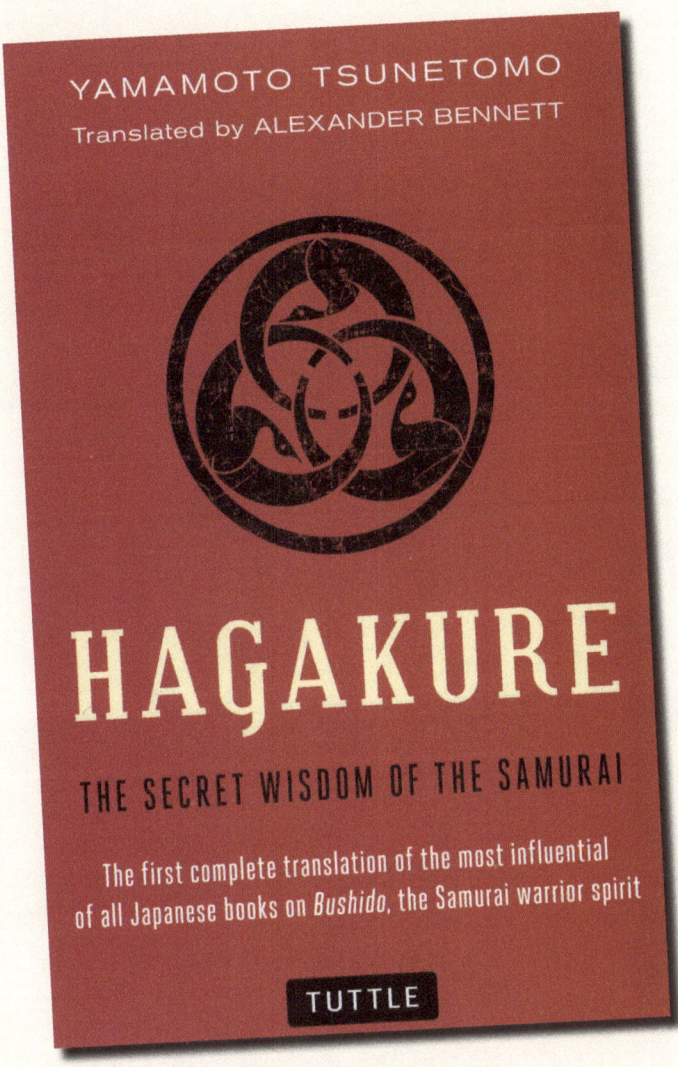

"Alex Bennett has produced the first truly authoritative translation and analysis of Hagakure—perhaps the most famous text ever written about samurai honor—to appear in any Western language. Simultaneously erudite and accessible, this volume belongs on the bookshelves of anyone—scholar or hobbyist alike—interested in samurai culture, or modern perceptions thereof."

— Dr. Karl F. Friday, author of *Samurai, Warfare and the State in Early Medieval Japan* and *Japan Emerging: Premodern History to 1850*

"[Alex Bennett] is the very best writer on martial arts alive today and [his] work needs to be showcased to the general public."

— Don Warrener, President, *Budo International*

"Dr. Bennett possesses a profound knowledge of, and deep insight into, the world of Japanese bushido. This expertise has been enhanced by his extensive practical experience of the traditional martial arts of Japan, and his proficiency in this domain is highly acclaimed."

— Tetsuo Yamaori, former Director of the International Research Center for Japanese Studies

"[A] strong point is a scholarly and succinct introduction that grounds the work in historical and social context, equipping the reader with a cultural map of Yamamoto's world. Footnotes provide valuable background and add resonance throughout, keeping names and familial relations straight, highlighting pertinent cross-references and generally rendering the work accessible to contemporary readers."

— *The Japan Times*

Search for "Bennett" and "Hagakure" on Amazon.com

Hagakure and the Ideal of Preparedness

by Alex Bennett

In my previous article, I introduced relevant martial art teachings from *Hagakure*, a classic treatise on bushido completed in 1716. *Hagakure* provides a fascinating window into the world of the samurai in Pax Tokugawa (1600-1868). This was an age in which glory earned in battle had become a distant memory for most, but the importance of overcoming the fear of death, and accepting its imminence, remained a central concern in the samurai ethos. Even in peacetime, nurturing the psychological strength to come to grips with one's mortality remained interwoven in the theoretical fabric of the Japanese martial arts. *Hagakure* provides us with hints as to how the samurai dealt with this concern.

Last time I discussed the idea of "*zanshin*"—literally "lingering mind", or constant mental and physical awareness. In this article, I will look at how *Hagakure* describes another ideal mindset in the daily life of the samurai: to always be prepared for the worst case scenario.

As the orator Yamamoto Jōchō advises, "With regards to the way of death, if you are prepared to die at any time, you will be able to meet your release from life with equanimity. As calamities are usually not as bad as anticipated beforehand, it is foolhardy to feel anxiety about tribulations not yet endured. Just accept that the worst possible fates for a man in service are to become a *rōnin*, or death by *seppuku*. Then nothing will faze you." (1-92) As long as you are already resigned to the worst possible thing that can happen to you, then it will not be a bother any more. Fear will not hinder you as you navigate your way through life being prepared to fall at any given moment.

This is an almost existential attitude, and Jōchō advocates the importance of never becoming confused in the face of a meaningless or absurd world. "Are men not like masterfully controlled puppets?" he asks. "It is magnificent craftsmanship that allows us to walk, jump, prance, and speak even though there are no strings attached. We may be guests at next year's Bon festival [for the dead]. We forget it is an ephemeral world in which we live." (2-45) For this reason, living with single-minded resolve, always being ready for whatever fate awaits you is, Jōchō asserts, the mindset of a "heroic warrior", and is the only way a samurai can liberate himself from his fleeting existence. He also warns that if you think of the seven days of hardship that lie ahead, it will most likely make you lose hope. If, however, you take things one day at a time, then the burden is but 1/7. This particular piece of advice has

got me through many a rigorous kendo training camp!

He also advises that the "prepared warrior" is not only able to solve problems in a quick and commendable fashion by virtue of his life experience, but he can also react appropriately through his comprehension of measures to meet any scenario. He is always ready. In contrast, "The unprepared warrior lacks foresight, and even if he succeeds in solving a problem, it is merely through good fortune rather than good planning. A warrior who doesn't think things through beforehand will be ill-equipped." (1-21)

Expressed in less dramatic terms, advice proffered in a quaint little vignette about the weather has served me well in Japan's rainy season due to my penchant of forgetting to take an umbrella. Perhaps this reflects a glaring lack of preparation in itself, but in any case there is a profound lesson to be learned from a downpour of rain. "If you get caught in a sudden cloudburst, you will still get a drenching even though you try to keep dry by hurrying along and taking cover under overhangs of roofs. If you are prepared to get wet from the start, the result is still the same but it is no hardship. This attitude can be applied to all things." (1-71)

Yet another teaching, which is just as, if not more, profound, involves how one engages in the decision-making process. "Deliberate lightly when deciding on weighty matters." This seems to go against the conventions of common sense, but it is followed up with an analysis that seems even more confused. "Be meticulous when deciding on affairs of minor importance." (1-46)

What can this possibly mean? The moral of this recommendation is that important matters are few in number, and can be studied carefully in the course of daily affairs. From this, it is meant that it is prudent to prepare for serious matters ahead of time so that they can be managed expediently. In other words, it is difficult to make quick and accurate decisions without planning in advance, and it is doubtful whether appropriate action can be taken as a result. To think lightly when deciding on weighty matters, is essentially to envisage issues of critical importance well before it has occurred, and to be prepared for the worst…

K8-dan Roberto Kishikawa-sensei's Kendo Seminar in São Carlos, Brazil
(November, 2015)

Carolina Akemi Martins Morita
Gil Vicente Nagai Lourenção
Kenji Nakahara Rocha
Yashiro Yamamoto

The Kishikawa seminar took place between November 21 and 28, 2015, in São Carlos in the state of São Paulo, Brazil. It was Roberto Kishikawa-sensei's first invitation to teach in Brazil after obtaining his 8-dan in Japan in November 2013. During the first weekend, about 140 kenshi from 12 dojo around Brazil were given the opportunity to learn from and talk to him. During the following week, he visited other dojo in Campinas, a city near São Carlos, and São Paulo city at the Kishikawa family dojo, where he conducted seminars for practitioners in the state of São Paulo.

In the evening of the first day, there was a celebration held in Kishikawa-sensei's honour. Also in attendance were dignitaries from several Brazilian kendo associations, not to mention his relatives and friends. He received a commemorative plate dedicated to him and São Carlos Kendo Association's 10th Anniversary. He was also given a special mention from São Carlos' City Council. During the event, Kishikawa-sensei and the other attendees watched various Japan-Brazil presentations and ate delicious *feijoada*—a typical Brazilian stew with beans and meat.

On the evening of Sunday, November 28, the last day of training, the traditional year-end party was convened by the São Carlos Kendo Association. Participants had the chance to socialise with each other, as well as to ask questions and converse with Kishikawa-sensei.

***

In countries where kendo is emerging, people are making great efforts toward its dissemination and development. It should therefore come as no surprise

when these countries start to gain international prominence in the mid- to long-term.

According to Kishikawa-sensei, we should aim for continued development and improvement in kendo achieved through the correct mindset and practice, not only individually, but also as an organisation. This should happen on an individual basis, when the practitioners themselves are able to critically discern the appropriate training for each specific stage. In Kishikawa-sensei's opinion, individual development should be guided by the following aim: How to score a valid strike (*ippon*). At each particular stage in a kendoka's development, one should be able to notice and understand:

1. What is considered an *ippon* at that stage?
2. How can we score an *ippon*?
3. How should we train to be able to score an *ippon*?

In effect, it is very important to take into consideration that the criteria used to evaluate an *ippon* changes according to each stage of one's development. If those differences are understood, training can be tailored taking into consideration degree and level, age, or personal goals. A similar understanding and flexibility can also be applied during *shiai*, as we should be able to adapt our behaviour and approach according to the circumstances and a particular moment.

It is therefore essential to have a clear personal goal, even though it might be constantly subject to change and re-evaluation. Seeking personal growth may be a better way to improve in kendo than short-period or status-centred goals. For instance, many athletes lose motivation after achieving a certain rank or title, as that was their final aim. However, when you pursue constant improvement and challenges, these achievements simply become what you acquire along the way, keeping you motivated.

For example, as a competitor Kishikawa-sensei never felt it would be right to face the World Kendo Championships in a frivolous manner. On the contrary, he always felt very committed to do his utmost and make the best of such opportunities. Before or after matches he always tried to also observe other *shiai* and the training methods of opposing teams and dojo. He was always looking for different ideas for continual advancement. Furthermore, whenever possible he would also take opportunities to train during his travels. This way, his participation in competitions was always part of his larger pursuit, but not the final aim itself.

Indeed, the athlete should be flexible in practice and when facing people they meet. There are plenty of styles, either in fighting or training, and each one is related to a unique context, individual, and goal. Many of them may be useful at some point in our own training, and inevitably we will come into contact with different methodologies during our development. We should always be open-minded about new contacts and approaches, and train in a thoughtful way with the clear intention of personal improvement. Reflection and the search for improvement should also be present when teaching. A teacher has to be constantly mindful of new possibilities. It is also necessary to be very clear with communication when training, teaching, or sharing experiences. Sometimes what we have to transmit is very delicate or hard to learn, so being honest and transparent is essential to avoid misunderstandings.

Last but not least, one must not forget the importance of the bonds developed during *keiko*. These are not restricted to the physical boundaries and schedule of the dojo. Socialising is also very rewarding and enriching. The importance of getting to know your training partners and sharing moments and stories beyond the training hours can't be overstated. Such bonds are essential not only for our own improvement, and also for the group and the practice itself.

Training

Kishikawa-sensei showed us that it is possible to practice *suriashi* footwork as well as *fumikomi* in the sand. Sand is a very unstable and irregular surface that absorbs impact and body propulsion. This exercise helped us to train more intensively while keeping our posture stable, and also enabled us to acquire hip and leg strength. Such training can overstrain the muscles a little, so it should not be practised for too long. On the other hand, it will only start to show results with time, so perseverance and dedication is needed.

Athletes put a lot of emphasis on speed, particularly when they are young, and therefore focus their training, movements and strategies around this aspect. The practitioner should be careful, however, not to neglect other skills that will become more important later. Speed will lose out in the end to other factors:

1. The pursuit of the best striking opportunity.
2. The search for the most efficient movement.
3. The refinement of your own criteria concerning *ippon*, considering its strength and precision.
4. Engaging in bouts in a more holistic way; that is, not only focusing on the instantaneous moment of the strike, but also the psychological build up.

We must always remember that psychological aspects play a crucial part in training, competing, and self-development. Sometimes, the difficulty of attempting a certain movement, or facing a particular opponent may be due to emotional factors rather than physical or technical deficiencies. For this reason, absolute concentration is an essential element in a contest, but it is less an innate talent than an ability honed through dedicated training.

In general, most kendoka lose focus when preoccupied with getting an *ippon*. They become fast and able to identify many opportunities during a fight, but end up only "hitting" the target without the full spirit and appropriate intensity required for an *ippon*. Needless to say, this is disadvantageous and will affect the kendoka's performance in high-level competitions, or when facing more experienced and higher-level opponents.

Consequently, many change their original purpose during training or competition, preferring to prioritise quick and easy results to the detriment of achieving a correct *ippon*. For instance, when facing a sensei, sempai or a strong opponent, it is common for the practitioner to start by trying to achieve a correct *ippon* in a focused manner, but if they do not accomplish their goal in the first few exchanges, they tend to resort to tricks like changing posture, and then compromise their elegance of movement and psychological stability. This means that they start worrying more about hitting their opponent at any cost instead of really trying to score a true *ippon*.

Some practitioners think only of not being struck by their opponent, forgetting that they are already protected by *bōgu* and the use of *shinai*, and that being stuck is a great way to learn. At worst, you may concede an *ippon*, but you can continue fighting—not like in the samurai era. We should appreciate the opportunity we have in kendo to learn how not to be conquered by our own fears.

Finally, we asked Kishikawa-sensei about etiquette, movements and kendo terms. In Brazil, we often come into contact with variations and new observations about different aspects of kendo. For instance, to initiate meditation, there are some who say that the instruction should be, "*Shisei wo tadashite, mokusō!*", ("Correct your posture! Meditate!") while there are others who say that calling only "*Seiza!*" is enough. Other variations include the different naming of some strikes, such as "*gyaku-dō*" which has recently been officially designated as "*migi-dō*". Then, there are variations involving the practice of the Nippon Kendo Kata. Kishikawa-sensei explained to us that there are rules that must be followed, as they are the real basis of kendo. However, there are other aspects that are

more flexible and subject to change, as even in Japan there is no general consensus. Actually, many high-level instructors occasionally propose adjustments to procedures, or sometimes create some conceptions and rules that better suit their own approach to kendo. Thus, while some superficial variations may be very personal, we should never forget that the fundaments of kendo must be correct and clear.

Some key points of guidance given during the seminar:

1. The dojo must be cleaned with a *zōkin*, a cleaning cloth, before and after training. Kishikawa-sensei asked us to bring our own *zōkin* so that we could do this during the seminar.
2. Each kenshi has to decide what he or she expects to achieve within kendo. As kendo is a way of self-development, the practitioner must be conscious of what he or she seeks so that progress toward that goal can be made.
3. Each kenshi also has to make time to practise alone. They must practise *suburi* and increase physical awareness. This *suburi* has to be applied in training in the same way that *kihon* is studied. For this reason, it is important to then establish a study routine to think about how *kihon* can be applied to *shiai*.
4. *Seme* is not about what you do, but rather about what your opponent feels. *Seme* is not only about attack; it is a way of destabilising the opponent. The opponent must feel your pressure, and if they do not, it is because there was no real and effective *seme*.
5. *Maai* must be developed and *kiai* should be understood as being about energy. *Maai* is the real distance between two opponents, and *kiai* is the manifestation of the physical energy involved in the bout.
6. Practitioners should realise that when they are not breathing in and out, that is, when the breath can be held, they will be able to strike. During their development, they should also seek the most effective use of their breath.
7. We must continuously strive to make the perfect *ippon*. Furthermore, analysing and understanding the reasons why a strike was or was not *ippon* will aid our development.

8. Always try to improve. Today must be better than yesterday; tomorrow must be better than today. Progress should not be measured by comparison with others, but by considering one's own circumstances.
9. The kenshi should try to apply the concepts of the "life-giving sword" (*katsujinken*) as opposed to the "life-taking sword" (*satsujinken*). For further information on these concepts, you can consult the *Heihō Kadensho* by Yagyū Munenori.
10. Look for the harmony of body, mind and spirit.
11. Fully concentrate on striking without worrying too much about being struck.
12. When practising kendo, it is important to know how to strike, and also how to be struck.
13. Learn to correctly apply what you have studied and practised.
14. Understand why the opponent is able to strike you and search for improvement.
15. Understand that *men*, the most difficult strike, is the one that must be practised most.
16. Know that rather than winning, what really matters is to feel satisfied with your performance in a match, and to try your best.
17. Know that in the future you may become an example for other practitioners. Therefore, you should try to compete and act correctly, both inside and outside the dojo.
18. Know that what really matters is to win over your own self, rather than to win against others.
19. Always try to give 100 percent at every moment, in each strike, *suburi*, *kihon*, *keiko* and *shiai*.
20. An *ippon* involves hitting the *datotsubu* with the correct *hasuji*, making the strike with *ki-ken-tai-itchi*, and then demonstrating *zanshin*.
21. An *ippon* is not solely dependent on your own skill or speed; it involves an interaction between you and your opponent.
22. Try not to strike at random without paying attention to the moment. To concentrate on scoring an *ippon* involves observing your opponent, finding the best opportunity to strike, and the best *waza* to use.
23. Think of every moment as a case of "sink or swim". This is why the *shinai* should be thought of as a real sword, and a match as a life-and-death situation. You should not have any doubts or fears.

Musō Jikiden Eishin-ryū Riai
The Meaning of the Kata: Part 4
By Kim Taylor

Introduction

This is Part 4 of a series of articles about the meaning behind the *kata* of the Musō Jikiden Eishin-ryū (MJER) and the organisation of those *kata* into their levels and order. I claim no special knowledge of the thoughts of Ōe Masamichi as I was not alive when he reorganised the school into its present order. I simply offer my thoughts on this from a background of 30 years of practice in this school and in some other Japanese sword arts. Please understand while you are reading this that this is one person's way of organising and understanding the material. You are encouraged to read this, compare it with what you have been taught and what you understand, and come to your own conclusions.

The Third Level: Oku Iai

The first three articles in this series looked at the *kata* of the Ōmori-ryū and Eishin-ryū, but now the focus moves to Oku Iai. Oku Iai contains seated and standing *kata*, and this article will examine the Oku Iai Iwaza (seated) techniques.

Oku Iai is where the practitioner is introduced to multiple attackers and continuous attacks. As was suggested at the end of the Eishin-ryū article, the practitioner has the grammar and the vocabulary, and can now speak in whole sentences. For this very reason, the Oku Iai probably should not be described in too much detail—it should be left to the sensei and student to fill in the gaps. This article will not go too far into the fine tuning of the *kata* that follow, nor will it examine the amazing number of variations that can be performed. Again, "ask your sensei".

The Oku Iai *kata* require a higher level of skill: a shorter and faster *nōtō* (the left hand makes contact with the back of the sword at the *monouchi*), sharper targeting, and more *enzan-no-metsuke* (a gaze that takes in the entire scene rather than focusing on one thing), which is needed to deal with multiple attackers. Other level-specific differences like those already mentioned can also be introduced to further challenge the practitioner and refine his or her abilities.

If it is assumed these are the oldest *kata*, it makes sense that both seated and standing *kata*, which are in fact similar to each other, are included. While the school is

Nōtō

Kasumi—front

Kasumi—side

Kasumi

assumed to have developed from Oku to Eishin to Ōmori, the student encounters the *kata* in reverse order. It seems that introductory, basic level *kata* have been added over the years in preparation for the originals. As an instructor, remember this difference between development and encounter when teaching beginners—keep the more basic movements of the earlier levels. It does not do anybody any favours to try to teach beginners the refinements of Oku Iai along with the "foot goes here" approach of the Ōmori-ryū.

Many techniques in this set are actually quite simple but they are performed quickly and continuously with angled cuts and the consideration of environmental factors. They are simple but not easy to perform. There will not be a great deal of discussion on how these are performed, but rather the focus will be on what they mean to the overall instruction in the school.

Oku Iai Iwaza

There are eight seated (*iwaza*) *kata* in this set.

Fluid Attack and Defence

The following two *kata* are largely review. However, by introducing multiple attacks and defences, it allows the practitioner to examine fluid movements from attack to attack and defence to attack.

1. Kasumi

Once again a set begins with a review of Mae, but this time a return cut is introduced as well as the concept of moving forward while making multiple cuts. The first cut from the *saya* is done with the right foot moving forward, like in Mae or Yoko Gumo. The second, return cut is done with a slide forward of the rear knee, and the final vertical cut with a step out once more of the right foot. This movement is simple but effective and allows multiple targeting while chasing. The shift up of the rear knee before the final cut is a characteristic of the Musō Shinden-ryū and the All Japan Kendo Federation *iai*.

Going back to the Eishin-ryū (see *Kendo World* 8.1) or forward to Sune Gakoi (the following *kata*), this could be seen as a response by the attacker to the block in Tora no Issoku. As the attacker in Tora no Issoku, once the shoulder is out of range, do not drop the tip to try and hit the knee. Instead let the opponent block too low and to the outside of the leg as you carry on past and return to cut the inside of their leg. This is the concept of a continuous attack.

Sune Gakoi—front

Sune Gakoi—side

Sune Gakoi

2. Sune Gakoi

This is a review of Tora no Issoku, but it is here so that we can examine the matching of this *kata* with Kasumi. There are two ways to deal with this problem of a continuous attack to both sides of the knee.

1. Sweep the block from the outside of the knee to the inside as the return cut is made by the attacker. Once that deflection is made, continue around behind the body, dropping to the knee and strike from above. This is as the *kata* is done in Tora no Issoku.

2. After the first block, drive the tip immediately toward the attacker's face to stop the return cut. This is a continuous defence, which is somewhat different than the defence in Tora no Issoku, or even Yae Gaki, and it is the way *kata* are practised in the Oku Iai level.

To Zume

Multiple Attackers

The next three *kata* introduce the idea of the environment in relation to the *kata*, and the idea that the practitioner might have to deal with multiple opponents.

3. To Zume

For the first time, the practitioner faces multiple attackers. We also see our first angled cut. (The final cut in Uke Nagashi is a *kesa-giri*, but the attacker is bent over so the cutting line is actually vertical). In this *kata* the student faces a door that opens to reveal two attackers at the right and left front angles. The right front attacker is dealt with by a *kiri-tsuke* (an angled overhead cut direct from the *saya*). This cut must be angled because if it is direct, there would be a lift overhead and cut down (a timing of two beats). The one-handed strike is followed by a vertical two-handed strike on the second opponent after the sword is brought through an *uke-nagashi* type movement—the wrist is relaxed, the tip is left toward the first attacker and the *tsuka-gashira* is directed toward the second attacker to start the sword movement.

There is a large environmental component in this *kata* as the practitioner is asked to deal with the door which has been opened. The right foot and the body are shifted forward to prevent the doors from being closed again once the attack is made on the attacker.

The next new concept is the way of targeting the opponents. At the highest level of practice, the target is identified and the cut made while the second target is being identified. This means that the practitioner must accurately cut the first opponent while already looking at the second.

A new level of speed is also introduced in this *kata* with the practitioner being expected to have returned the blade into the *saya* with only about 10cm left exposed, by the time the first opponent hits the floor. A relaxed efficient movement must be learned in order for these *kata* to be done at this kind of speed.

To Waki

4. To Waki

The practitioner is now a guard outside a door sitting at a 45-degree angle to the wall—the most effective way to sit in a narrow hallway. The opponent to the rear left is thrust at, and the one to the front right is cut vertically in this *kata*.

The opponent to the rear left is attacked first simply because he must be closer and therefore the more dangerous of the two opponents. This opponent can be reached with an *ushiro-tsuki* movement. Using *seme*, the opponent to the front must be made to hesitate and the draw toward the front must convince him that he is the first target.

As the thrust is made to the rear before dealing with the opponent in front, there should be little time between the thrust and the cut.

The practitioner is now learning how to prioritise multiple targets: in To Zume we choose the attacker to the right because he can be cut directly from the scabbard and both are equal threats. In To Waki, as he is the greater threat, the closer opponent must be dealt with first by using a draw and thrust rather than attacking the attacker to the right. A smooth draw and turn of the hips can make this draw and thrust to the rear a one-beat attack instead of two.

Shiho Giri—front

Shiho Giri—rear

Shiho Giri—alternate

5. Shiho Giri

The practitioner now encounters four attackers in a *kata* that could easily be seen as an extension of To Waki. The attacker to the rear left is dealt with first as he is the greatest threat. The rest are dealt with in turn and according to their threat level.

This *kata* introduces the importance of keeping your sword above your head as much as possible when dealing with multiple attackers.

Tana Shita—front

Tana Shita—side

Simple Kata

While the following *kata* are not as complex as those of 4, 5, 6 or 9 in the Eishin-ryū, they are perhaps more difficult because they deal with multiple attackers and the influence of the environment on the techniques. It is not difficult to perform complex movements against a single opponent, but the mere existence of multiple attackers means that the practitioner cannot "get fancy". Strict control of *maai*, of timing and distance, is the only way to succeed.

6. Tana Shita

The environment is again important in this *kata* which starts under a veranda. This could also be any kind of low-ceilinged place where a cut must be made while clearing overhead obstructions. This *kata* also introduces a modification to the usual overhead cut, with a very flat and forward trajectory of the tip to avoid any obstructions. By moving out from under the veranda we can see how *tatehiza* can be used to cover a lot of ground.

Ryo Zume—front

Ryo Zume—side

7. Ryo Zume

This takes place in a narrow hallway with an opponent in front, and has a new way to draw, and a second thrust (to the front). The draw is made simply to put the blade in our hands in a *chūdan* position. However, drawing while threatening the opponent in order to allow the practitioner the time to reach *chūdan* and to thrust must be learned.

Tora Bashiri

8. Tora Bashiri

In Tora Bashiri there are multiple opponents and a crowd of bystanders as well. This *kata* teaches how to move through a crowd of people without tripping or stepping on them by taking small steps in line with each other. By placing the knees together (a posture secret in the higher levels of iaido and the set in which the practitioner wears a long tight skirt that restricts movements) we learn that this is possible.

As the practitioner moves back to create the distance needed for drawing against the second opponent, we learn the other side of the Omori-ryū technique, Oi Kaze.

The next article will look at the Oku Iai Tachiwaza—the standing forms.

Dojo Files

Current members and friends of Nenriki at the 50th Anniversary Meeting on March 12, 2016

Nenriki Dojo: 50 Years
Victor Harris

Since its inception in early 1966, the Nenriki Dojo has met every Tuesday and Friday evening during school term times at the Chaucer Institute (previously known as Trinity School) in Harper Road, London SE1, and currently convenes at Rockingham Community Centre in nearby Falmouth Road. Traditionally we also meet after every *keiko* at the aptly named Rising Sun pub, which boasts a long and distinguished history of more than a century.

The Nenriki Dojo was given its name by the late Hanshi, Dr. Itō Kyoitsu, founder of the Seijudo Dojo in Tokyo. It was at this dojo where our first teacher, Ōsaki Shintarō, practised kendo during his undergraduate years in the Department of Literature at Meiji University. Ōsaki underwent a two year course in Baking Technology from 1966 (the year of our founding) to 1968 at Borough Polytechnic, now South Bank University. The sports hall of South Bank University was the venue for the Nenriki Dojo 50th Anniversary celebrations on March 12, 2016, at which Ōsaki was guest of honour.

The Nenriki Dojo was established with the great support of Dr. Itō, the All Japan Kendo Federation, especially the late Hanshi Takizawa Kōzō, and the Japanese Foreign Office, with backing from leading British kendo practitioners including Roald Knutsen and our first President Charles Lidstone (d. 1970), in whose memory we host the annual *kyū* grade Lidstone Taikai.

During Ōsaki's time in London there were many visitors to Nenriki from Japan, among whom Fujii Okimitsu remains active today. He was entrusted with the keep of the dojo when Ōsaki returned to Japan. In turn, Fujii passed the responsibility to Victor Harris, the current president, who had also spent three years at the Seijudo in Japan.

A pillar of strength to both Nenriki and the British Kendo Association (BKA) in the years leading to the 3rd World Kendo Championships in 1976, was the late Kikuchi Kōichi-sensei of the Embassy of Japan, followed by several Japanese teachers who were on year-long sabbaticals. A number of Nenriki members from those early two years still remain active in kendo. In some cases they have moved away from London, or established new dojo, but are always regarded as members of the Nenriki (see photograph).

Furthermore, many prominent members of the BKA have given great support to Nenriki from the early 1970's, and several members from those days continue to work maintaining our aspiration of high level kendo study.

The role that Nenriki has played in the growth of the BKA is not well known. From among the Nenriki membership have emerged a number of teachers who formed other London clubs, starting with Mumeishi and Hagakure. Nenriki was also a founder member of the reformed BKA, and both the European Kendo Federation and International Kendo Federation.

Prominent members in the late 1960s
L to R: Jock Hopson, Len Bean, John Howell, Jean Paul Tuvi (visitor), the late Terry Holt, Mike Davies, Fujii Okimitsu

Nenriki has also always provided the BKA with officers in time of need, and supported international activities. The British directors, representatives, vice presidents, and presidents of the aforementioned associations have always been predominantly members of Nenriki, and who have in turn led the dojo, notably, in alphabetical order, Errol Baboolal Blake, Fujii Okimitsu, Victor Harris, Anthony Hopson, John Howell, Roald Knutsen and Tony and Tsuyaku Palmer. We have also been fortunate to have had many long term visiting teachers from Japan, too numerous to name here, who remain lifelong friends. Around the same time as the formation of Nenriki Dojo, Dr. Itō also named the Zanshin Dojo in Bristol. He gave us the calligraphy of the words "*nenriki*" and "*zanshin*" which is reproduced on both our *tenugui* and *zekken*.

In celebration of our 50th Anniversary, Ōsaki Shintarō prepared a commemorative *tenugui* with two characters of Japanese calligraphy "*fusho*" written by Dr. Itō Kyoitsu, with a dedication to his pupil Ōsaki written fifty years ago. The word "*fusho*" can be translated as "without hesitation". The three words "*nenriki*", "*fusho*", and "*zanshin*" can be thought of as the three requisites of "preparation, action, and conclusion". These are discussed in the booklet *Kendo and the Formation of the Human Being - A Record of the Sayings of the Late Ogawa Chutaro*, which was prepared for the fiftieth anniversary of the foundation of Setagaya-ku Kendo. This booklet was translated into English for the occasion of Nenriki's 45th Anniversary five years ago, the contents of which we endeavour to seek in our everyday practice.

Visitors are always welcome at Nenriki. Please confirm *keiko* times before visiting by sending a message to start@kendo.co.uk

Address: Rockingham Community Centre in nearby Falmouth Road, London SE1 6QP
Access: Nenriki is a close to Elephant & Castle and Borough underground stations

The Meaning of Nenriki

Loosely based on extracts from the 1966 publication *Nenriki* by the late Dr. Itoh Kyoitsu, the word "*nenriki*" is composed of two characters, "*nen*" and "*riki*". The second character "*riki*" means strength, or power, and has straightforward meanings when used in combination with many other characters. The first character "*nen*" is less easily definable, but has the following connotations according to the *Kakugawa Kanwa Chū Jiten* dictionary:

1. to think
2. to learn
3. to chant, or read
4. used as the number twenty in some applications
5. to moderate, take care, or refrain
6. an extremely short interval of time in Buddhism

According to a number of other dictionaries, the two characters together mean something like "the strength of resolution" or "the strength of single-mindedness". In Buddhism, "*nenriki*" can mean a spiritual strength brought about by chanting the "*Kannon kyo*" sutra, but it has different meanings according to other sutras. In an emergency, human beings are capable of exerting enormous strength over a short period of time. That strength can be nurtured through kendo training as "*nenriki*".

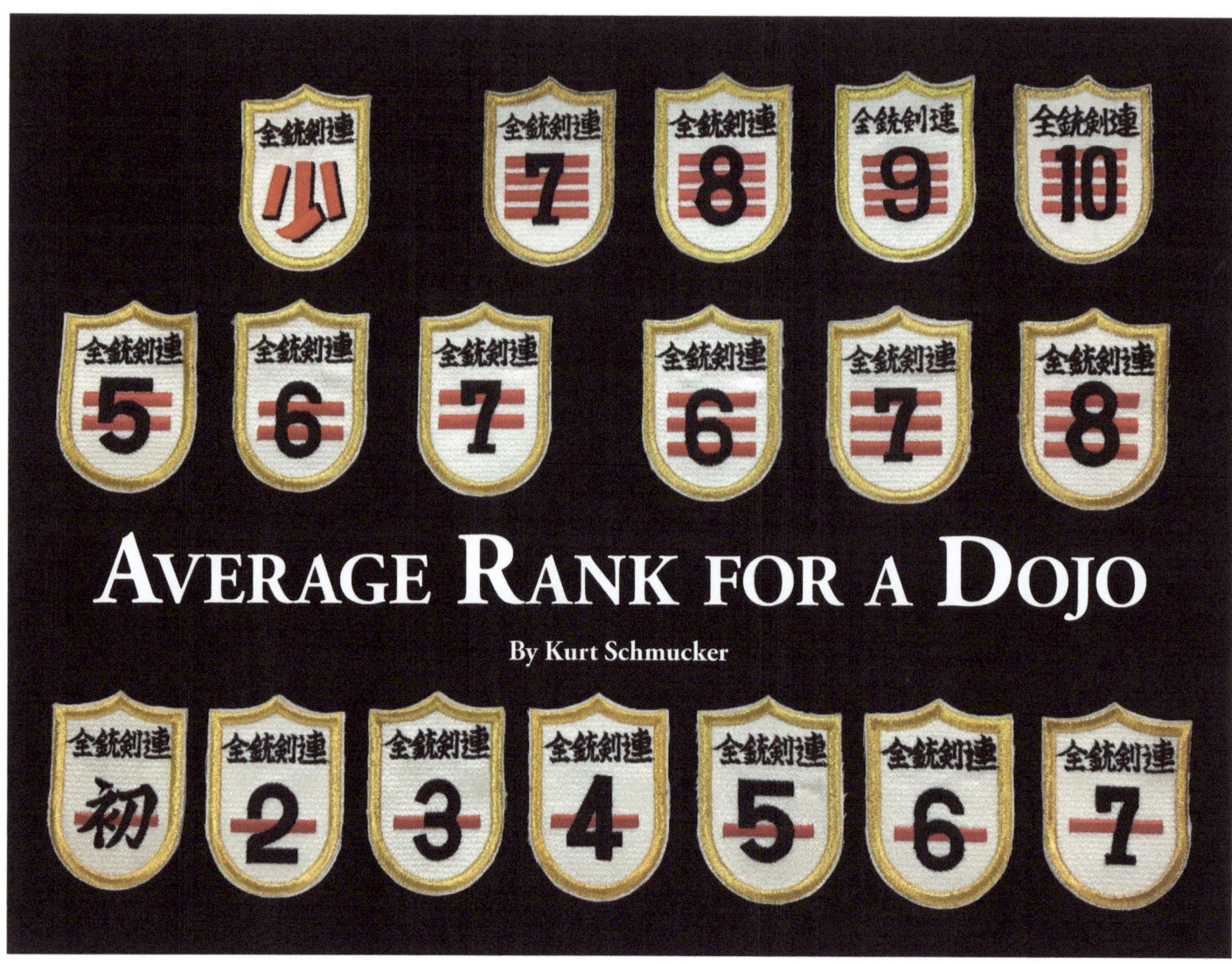

Average Rank for a Dojo

By Kurt Schmucker

What's the "average rank" of a dojo or other group? Consider these three fictitious kendo dojo, each with seven members:

Dojo A	Dojo B	Dojo C
One 6-dan	One 3-dan	One 5-dan
One 2-dan	Four Shodan	Three 4-dan
Three Shodan	Two 2-kyū	Three Shodan
Two 3-kyū		

Clearly, the "average rank" of Dojo A is greater than that of Dojo B, but what about Dojo C? Is the "average rank" of Dojo C higher or lower than that of Dojo A?

This article examines several ways of computing and comparing this notion of average rank, ways that are independent of individual arts (kendo, iaido, naginata, etc.) and can even be used to compare different arts. Any formula for calculating the average rank will have to include terms like this:

(Number of 5-dan holders) × (5-dan weight) +
(Number of 4-dan holders) × (4-dan weight) …

The real heart of the formula will be in the weights used.

Any easy set of weights will just be the numerical value of the *dan* or *kyū*. In effect, a piecewise linear scale.

Rank	8-dan	7-dan	6-dan	5-dan	4-dan	3-dan	2-dan	Shodan	Ikkyū
Weight	8	7	6	5	4	3	2	1	0.9

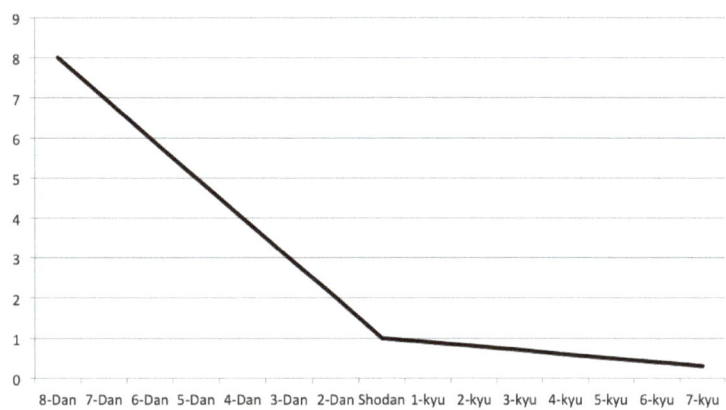

Figure 1. Piecewise linear weights

Using these weights, we get the average ranks for the three fictitious dojos:

Dojo A	Dojo B	Dojo C
1.77	1.22	2.85
Shodan+	Shodan	2-dan+

While easy to understand, the piecewise linear weights did not seem to take into account the many years of time in grade and the difficulty of the exams for the higher grades. Squaring the values produces almost a piecewise quadratic set of weights:

Rank	8-dan	7-dan	6-dan	5-dan	4-dan	3-dan	2-dan	Shodan	Ikkyū
Weight	64	49	36	25	16	9	4	1	0.81

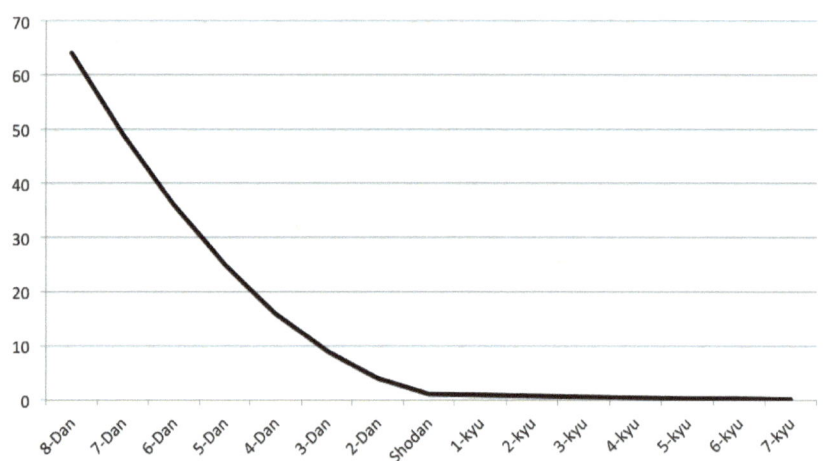

Figure 2. Piecewise quadratic weights

Using these new weights, we get the average ranks for the three fictitious dojo.

Dojo A
6.28
2-dan+

Dojo B
2.04
Shodan+

Dojo C
10.85
3-dan

These seem like better average ranks for the three dojo.

Shōgō titles

The *shōgō* titles — Renshi, Kyōshi, and Hanshi — add some additional points on the rank dimension. Numerically, I choose to place Renshi between 6-dan and 7-dan, Kyōshi between 7-dan and 8-dan, and Hanshi above 8-dan, though I realise that other placements could realistically be made.

The final set of weights I used is:

Rank	Hanshi	8-dan	Kyōshi	7-dan	Renshi	6-dan	5-dan	4-dan	3-dan	2-dan
Weight	72.25	64	56.25	49	42.25	36	25	16	9	4

Rank	Shodan	Ikkyū	2-kyū	3-kyū	4-kyū	5-kyū	6-kyū	7-kyū
Weight	1	0.81	0.64	0.49	0.36	0.25	0.16	0.09

The final calculation for the average rank of a dojo or group I used is:

$$rank_{avg} = \frac{\sum_{rank=7kyu}^{hanshi} holders_{rank} \times weight_{rank}}{\sum_{rank=7kyu}^{hanshi} holders_{rank}}$$

Figure 3. Average rank formula

Using the formula

So now that we have this formula, does it seem to match common sense? To see, I used the formula with three groups that I have rank data for: the Pacific Northwest Naginata Federation[1]—one of the six regional federations in the United States Naginata Federation; the Canadian Kendo Federation[2]; and the All Japan Kendo Federation[3].

Pacific Northwest Naginata Federation

The rank distribution of the PNNF is:

Rank	Hanshi	Kyōshi	Renshi	5-dan	4-dan	3-dan	2-dan	Shodan
People	0	0	1	2	0	4	1	1

Rank	Ikkyū	2-kyū	3-kyū	4-kyū	5-kyū	6-kyū
People	3	2	2	1	0	0

Note that naginata does not have dan ranks above 5-dan nor a 7-kyū, so those cells have been removed from the table.

Using the formula with the quadratic weights results in an average rank of 8.13, which is just a bit short of the weight for 3-dan, a level which seems about right.

Canadian Kendo Federation

The rank distribution of the CKF is:

Rank	Hanshi	8-dan	Kyōshi	7-dan	Renshi	6-dan	5-dan	4-dan	3-dan	2-dan
People	?	3	?	35	?	24	54	88	153	211

Rank	Shodan	Ikkyū	2-kyū	3-kyū	4-kyū	5-kyū	6-kyū	7-kyū
People	208	?	?	?	?	?	?	?

I was unable to obtain information about shōgō titles or kyū grades in the CKF, so these cells had to be ignored.

Using the formula with the quadratic weights results in an average rank of 9.74, which is a fraction above the weight for 3-dan, which also seems about right.

All Japan Kendo Federation

The rank distribution of the AJKF is:

Rank	9-dan	Hanshi	8-dan	Kyōshi	7-dan	Renshi	6-dan	5-dan	4-dan
People	4	?	662	?	16380	?	18516	48785	57269

Rank	3-dan	2-dan	Shodan	Ikkyū	2-kyū	3-kyū	4-kyū	5-kyū	6-kyū	7-kyū
People	243,534	545,487	814,090	?	?	?	?	?	?	?

Data on shōgō titles or kyū ranks in the AJKF was not able to be obtained, so those cells were ignored.

First, I had to add a weight for 9-dan, since the AJKF has four individuals with that grade. I have assigned the weight of 81 (9^2) for 9-dan.

Using the formula with the quadratic weights results in an average rank of 5.06, which is slightly above the weight for 2-dan. This seems too low, but perhaps the data on *shōgō* titles would raise this average. Just as likely, however, is that this formula, intended to calculate an average weight for a smaller group like a dojo or a smaller federation, does not scale for an organisation the size of the AJKF.

Endnotes

1. http://www.pnnf.org/
2. Data published on Power BI, courtesy of the Canadian Kendo Federation. http://bit.ly/21v7gRu - Accessed February 15, 2016.
3. Bennett, Alex. *Kendo: Culture of the Sword*. Oakland: University of California Press, 2015. p.xxxiv

Author bio

Kurt Schmucker teaches naginata in the Seattle area, and is the current president of the United States Naginata Federation. He holds the following ranks: naginata Renshi, iaido 5-dan, kendo 4-dan, jodo 3-dan, judo shodan and Shindō Musō-ryū Jōjutsu Oku-iri.

THE WILLIAM DE LANGE INTERVIEW

文武両道

The Dual Path of Sword and Brush

Over the past few years, William de Lange has made a great contribution to the body of English-language historical materials with numerous books including his biography Miyamoto Musashi: A Life in Arms *and his translations of Japanese source materials in* Origins of a Legend: Real Musashi I, II, & III *(published by Floating World Editions). The following interview was conducted by e-mail with Mr. de Lange from his home.*

Kendo World: Thank you so much for this interview. Can you start by telling us a bit about your background?

William de Lange: Yes, my father was Dutch and my mother English. He was an officer in the merchant navy; she was a stewardess—that's how they met, a very romantic time, especially during the fifties. When I was born they had already moved to Holland, so I was raised the Dutch way, although my mother made it a point to inculcate in my older brother and me the English traditions, her love of literature, Shakespeare, Sunday roasts, mince pies for Xmas. I suppose it was why I took up my English studies, though already after one year I quit my studies and left for Japan in search of adventure.

KW: How did you first become interested in Japan?

WdL: I can remember being totally fascinated by Kung Fu movies. At nine I had my mother buy me kimono-like pajamas and got my brother—who is very artistic—to decorate it with Chinese characters; it looked really cool. It made me feel like Kwai Chan Kaine. My first interest in Japan came with the TV adaption of Clavell's *Shogun*, starring Richard Chamberlain. I was utterly spellbound by the exotic culture, the samurai ethic, Japanese women, architecture, customs, clothing. I remember keeping a small book in which I meticulously recorded every Japanese phrase and expression that came up—that is now almost 40 years ago. I think that fascination lay dormant for the next ten years, until I enrolled in a Japanese language course while studying English at Groningen University (in the north of The Netherlands). I got so immersed in it that I quit my English studies after a year and booked a flight to Japan. That was in 1989, some 26 years ago.

KW: What was it like when you first arrived in Japan?

WdL: It was a wonderful experience: everything about the country fascinated me, the people, the language, the landscape, the culture, the food, the architecture, everything. I wanted to stay. I had made a demo tape of my music and went round all the major record labels in the hope of landing a contract but had no success. Teaching English was also difficult, as I did not have a Commonwealth passport, even though my mother was English. Eventually I ended up working for an acquaintance of my Japanese teacher. In retrospect not finding other employment was a blessing in disguise.

KW: Who was this acquaintance of your teacher?

WdL: The man, Teruo Takayanagi, was a traditional scroll maker (*hyōguya*), living and working in Mobara, Chiba prefecture. Sadly, he passed away last year. He was one of the best in his field, winning many awards, and was for many years the head of the association of scroll makers for his prefecture. I spent the next six months completely immersed in a traditional side of Japan I would otherwise never have discovered. We worked all over the place, met fascinating people and I learned a traditional craft that is fast disappearing, making not only scrolls, but also sliding doors, ornate folding screens, and paper screens.

Still, I began to worry about my education. Though I was rapidly learning Japanese, I had not completed my studies. I therefore decided to return home the next year and enter Leiden University to study Japanese in earnest. Going back was hard. I had come to love the place and found it difficult to leave everything behind.

KW: How did you get involved in iaido?

WdL: I spent one year of my studies at Waseda University on a scholarship from the Japanese Ministry of Education (*Monbusho*), and spent many more months during my holidays working for the scroll maker and absorbing the culture. It was during my study at Waseda that I saw an iaido demonstration by an old man at my dormitory. I was hooked. I immediately went up to him and asked him if I could come and practise with him. He turned out to be a descendant of an old *daimyō* clan, the Satake, and for the next ten months I spent my Tuesday and Thursday evenings practising Musō Shinden-ryū Iaido at the dojo of the Seijōgakuen-mae police station. Looking back, they were some of the happiest days of my life. I felt I was penetrating a world that was radically different from the one in which I had grown up and I loved every minute of it. Having practised other martial arts before, I was especially struck with the grace and composure of iaido. There was a certain concentrated power in the execution of the techniques that made me feel as if I were being transported right back into some feudal setting, populated by samurai who still lived by the bushido code, the only sound the rustling of their *hakama* and their sword as it cleaved the air.

The mystique soon vanished when I took up practising under Satake-sensei. As with so many of Japan's arts, it takes ages and ages before you even begin to scratch the surface of a technique. The first few times it feels like magic. But as you progress, you feel that every time you practise your execution of the technique becomes worse and worse, until you feel like hanging your sword in the top of the highest tree. What happens, of course, is that you become increasingly sensitised to every nuance of a technique and your own shortcomings—shortcomings of which you hadn't been aware the week before. Only through many years of training will you gradually master every nuance, forging them into a whole, and slowly but gradually feel that you're actually making progress.

KW: How did you come into contact with Shinkage-ryū?

WdL: After I graduated I returned to Japan and found work for a large robotics company near Nagoya, Aichi prefecture. My old teacher in Tokyo suggested I take up practising the Shinkage-ryū, as it was the traditional art of swordsmanship of Aichi province. So for the next four years I practised under Hanshi 8-dan Akita Moriji-sensei and his protégé Matsuoka Yoshitaka-sensei. Of course, it was back to square one when I started. The Shinkage-ryū is profoundly

At home with a befriended sword aficionado

different from the Musō Shinden-ryū in that in many of its techniques you remain partly squatting. This puts an enormous strain on the upper legs (a bit as in skiing) and makes it terribly difficult to execute a technique with the same controlled composure as if one were standing or sitting. Once you do master this style of fencing, it gives you tremendous added control over the whole sequence of a technique from sitting, to squatting, to standing. I began to gather material on the Shinkage-ryū and in my spare time I began writing a book that was eventually published by Weatherhill under the title *Iaido: The History, Teachings, and Practice of Japanese Swordsmanship*.

KW: What do you see as the value of practising traditional martial arts?

WdL: Your question is a really good one. I think the answer will differ from practitioner to practitioner. To me it is was initially a means to penetrate Japan's deep-rooted cultural traditions—a means to better understand the Japanese psyche. Yet I have come to believe that to practise a Japanese martial art is to train the spirit more than anything else. If you want to learn effective ways of besting your opponent, you'd better go on a Navy Seal training course. If you want to master your own weaknesses and gain profound insight into your own strengths and weaknesses, there is no better way than to follow in the steps of the old *musha shūgyōsha*. It is probably for that reason that I decided to stop practising when I returned to Europe some ten years ago. I wanted to turn to the one thing I had always wanted to do: write books on Japan.

KW: How did you start your writing career?

WdL: My first book naturally followed from my thesis, in that I expanded it into a history of Japanese journalism from the late Edo period up until the postwar American occupation. At that time the main challenge was still the Japanese source material, much of which was in the staid, formal prewar Japanese, with sentences that run on for half a page. Even more challenging were the texts from earlier periods. This is especially true for texts on the martial arts, which of course was a huge subject for medieval Japanese and already had my interest. I had studied classical Japanese at university, but as you know, there are so many terms and expressions even unfamiliar to a Japanese that it took a long time before I felt at home in this area. Even now I run into expressions that throw you completely at first. Then, with patience, a lot of research and asking Japanese experts, you finally get it. "Understanding is the point at which the mind comes at rest," my professor used to say—he was so right. My frustration at the lack of idiomatic reference material finally led me to compile a dictionary on Japanese idioms, and later one on Japanese proverbs. It was a bit of a slog, but well worth it, as I can now look up a term or proverb in my own dictionaries!

KW: How, or why, did you decide to tackle the life story of Miyamoto Musashi?

WdL: The how and why are closely connected. When I became hooked on iaido I began to read the standard works on Japanese swordsmen, Tsukahara Bokuden, Iizasa Chōisai Ienao, Kamiizumi no Kami

Nobutsuna, and of course Miyamoto Musashi. I soon found that there were major discrepancies between the Japanese and English sources. Especially in Musashi's case the differences stood out. I think the major reason for this was the success of Yoshikawa Eiji's novel *Musashi*, which was not only a huge hit in Japan in the years leading up to World War II, but also in the West in the decades after.

From a writer's point of view, I completely understand Yoshikawa Eiji [and the fictional changes he made]: he lets Musashi bite the dust in one of the most epic battles of Japanese medieval history. From a historian's perspective Eiji's choice was less fortunate. Largely due to the popularity of his work, many Western historians have come to assume that Musashi indeed fought among the losing forces in that famous battle. There are many more such instances, which is borne out beautifully by the Japanese and English entries for Musashi on Wikipedia, which on many points are almost diametrically opposed. To counter the distortion caused by Yoshikawa's brilliant work I had to go back to the original sources to reconstruct Musashi's life.

One more reason for me to do so was the myth that, next to Musashi's own writings there were no original sources to speak of. To my great surprise and delight, I soon found that there was a wealth of original sources, most of which had never been published in English before. Thus I set about to translate the two-dozen medieval Japanese texts in which Musashi makes his appearance, ranging from original accounts of battles, sieges, duels, local histories and topographies, clan records, and roll calls. The result was a body of text comprising 150,000 words, which has meanwhile been published in the three-part series *The Real Musashi: Origins of a Legend*.

It was only when I had completed this work, which took me a decade, that I felt confident to write a full biography on Musashi. The ambition of the three-part series had been to collect and translate all the original sources that were available, a kind of database with extensive annotations for anyone who wanted to go to the source material directly. Writing a biography, by contrast, would allow me to present a portrait of Musashi that I believed would most accurately reflect the man's course through life, his battles, his duels, his beliefs, his interests, his extraordinary talents, as well as his shortcomings. It took me three more years to write the biography, which has been published under the title *Miyamoto Musashi: A Life in Arms*.

KW: After all those years studying and translating, what kind of man do you think Musashi was? He is enigmatic, and paradoxical because he was obviously a violent man but is also respected as having been a very enlightened man.

WdL: I think he was a genius in his own right, but like many brilliant men he was also a flawed character whose single-minded pursuit of victory at all costs at times marred his reputation. I also think that in spite of all his successes he was not as supremely confident as some might believe, especially toward the other sex. For one, he was not the most handsome of samurai, being a long-time sufferer from eczema, which in those days was associated with bad karma. Yet it seems to me that much of his insecurity—as well as his burning desire to succeed and his refusal to enter anyone's service—can be traced to his deeply troubled relationship with his father, Muni, who expelled Musashi from his house when he was only eight years old. Yet to find out more about that, you'll have to read the biography...

Man's capacity to stoop to the most depraved barbarism while at the same time rising to the most exalted of arts remains one of the great riddles that lie at the core of humanity. Don't get me wrong. I believe that Musashi had a solid moral core and never stooped *that* low. Yet he does pose the paradox of artistic sensitivity combined with martial brutality. We mustn't indeed forget that he lived in a very violent age, where the life of a common man was worth little. Yet I strongly believe that the philosopher in him recognised this almost schizophrenic aspect in himself—and in so many other cultured warriors. I think it is why it was so common in those days for warriors to take the tonsure at the end of their military careers.

KW: Musashi seems to be one of the people who best embodies the ideal of "Bun Bu Ryo-do" or the dual path of learning and martial arts. You have also studied martial arts intensely while writing, studying languages, and learning traditional Japanese arts like

Following an enbu photo-shoot with Matsuoka Yoshitaka-sensei and Kinomoto Miyuki-sensei

scroll-making. What role does Bun-Bu Ryodo play in your life?

WdL: I suppose that, in general, I learned from my parents that you should always try to get a balance between the two. When I was small, they reminded me not to neglect my studies if I was out playing all day. Later, when I took up studying, they impressed on me the importance of physical exercise, as well as mental—not that they were in any way influenced by Asian concepts; to them it was just sound common sense. It was partly for that reason that I took up practising martial arts when I was at university.

We did a lot of classical text during my time at Leiden University. One text was by the eighteenth century Confucianist samurai-scholar Saitō Setsudō called *Shidō yōron*. I was impressed by Setsudō's clarity of thought and the insight he provided into the mindset of the Tokugawa samurai, and quoted his work extensively in my first book on iaido. The *Shidō yōron* is made up of six chapters titled: Duty, Manners, Spirit, Fidelity, Benevolence, and The Way. And it is in that last chapter that I first came across the dual concept of *bun* and *bu*, the dual way of the civil and the martial. "Learning and the practice of military arts," Setsudō writes, "must be pursued side by side; this is the first rule of the *Buke sho-hatto*."

The *Buke sho-hatto*, a collection of edicts issued in 1615 by the newly installed Tokugawa shogunate was drafted more than two centuries before Setsudō put brush to paper, which goes to show that the Tokugawa authorities put great stock in the concept. The *Buke sho-hatto* was revised several times over the following centuries, and it so happens that the hero of the current book I'm working on was the driving force behind the second, most important revision of 1635. That man was Yagyū Munenori, patriarch of the famous Yagyū clan, and the only man in Japanese feudal history who rose to the rank of *daimyō* through his mastery of the sword.

My book deals with the full history of the Yagyū clan, an eventful and at times traumatic one. Living through times of great upheaval, the Yagyū were first and foremost warriors who lived and survived by the sword. Yet throughout their long history you can see that they always adhered to the dual way of *bun* and *bu*, even in their darkest hours.

KW: We are looking forward to reading that as soon as it becomes available. Thank you for your time and thank you again for your many wonderful books which have shed so much light on the history of medieval Japanese budo.

J-Concepts' Samurai Green Tea
Samurai Green Tea

Traditional Green Tea from Makinohara City, Shizuoka Prefecture, Japan

ADVERTISEMENT

The Samurai Green Tea Fundraising System

No matter how much we love kendo, the costs involved in it can at times put a strain on even the deepest of wallets. Buying a quality set of *bōgu* can require a big financial commitment, and we've all spent good money on a *shinai* only for it to break after a few training sessions. An even greater expense are the costs involved in travelling to major competitions.

With the exception of kendoka from the major kendo countries such as Japan, Korea and the U.S., many competitors receive little or no financial support from their federation and will have to largely pay their own way to compete in major competitions like the WKC. In order to help meet the costs of travel, some competitors or federations will undertake activities like sponsored *suburi-athons*. It is also difficult for small clubs and federations to purchase the equipment necessary to carry out their activities. With these issues in mind, J-Concepts and Kendo World have collaborated to bring you the Samurai Green Tea Fundraising System to help you raise money for your club, federation or competition travel expenses.

So what exactly is the Samurai Green Tea Fundraising System and how can it help you?

First, Samurai Green Tea comes from Makinohara City in Shizuoka prefecture. This is the heart of Japan's "tea country", and is an area synonymous with the finest green tea. Strongly linked to kendo, this tea actually comes from plantations founded by samurai-come-tea grower, Chūjō Kageaki, whose fascinating story is in the following pages. One canister of Samurai Green Tea contains 20 freshly-packed teabags that can be used to make hot or cold tea. You would order a minimum of one pack of 24 canisters of Samurai Green Tea for $312, which includes postage to anywhere in the world. This works out to be $13 per canister. Next, sell them at the RRP of $19.95, and the profit you make can then go towards paying for travelling expenses, new club *bōgu*, or whatever it is that you need to raise money for.

Seito Kenyukai Original Label

A unique feature of this product is that you are able to personalise it. Create your own label from scratch or use one of our templates. Once you have placed an order and submitted the label artwork, the tea will be picked and packed, and then labels will be affixed to the canisters. You will receive your totally original canisters of Samurai Green Tea 10–20 days later.

1. Contact Graham, your tea and fundraising consultant, at tea@kendo-world.com to see how Samurai Green Tea can help you realise your goal.

2. Design your own label to the required size.

2. Choose one of the many templates and decide what text or photos to use.

3. Submit the label data with your order* and make payment.
   * A minimum order is one carton (24 canisters of 20 tea-bags for $312 including postage to anywhere in the world).

4. Once payment is received, labels will be printed and affixed to canisters.

5. Your tea will then be freshly packed, off the tree not the shelf.

6. Once your product is ready it will be dispatched by international courier.

7. Your carton of customised canisters of tea will arrive 10 to 20 days after confirmation of order depending on your zone. (Delivery times to South America and Africa will take slightly longer.)

8. Sell at the RRP of $19.95 to make $166.80 per carton towards your goal!

9. Still need to raise more funds?

10. No. Buy more tea because it tastes great!

10. Yes. Then buy more tea!

Of course, Samurai Green Tea need not only be bought for fundraising. It can also be used as a commemorative gift to give to friends or family.

Members of Canterbury Kendo Club that were selected to represent New Zealand at the 16th WKC in Tokyo used the Samurai Green Tea Fundraising System to help finance their trip to Japan. Here's what they had to say about it:

"The Samurai Green Tea was a low cost and hugely beneficial aspect of our fund raising efforts to get to the 16th WKC. The option to customise the label made it simple to sell to club members, family and friends. Additionally, as it is green tea, people needed little convincing of its practical value in comparison to other fund raising items we were selling."—Blake Bennett

"Fundraising has always been a tricky one for the Kendo Club. Over the years and campaigns, inevitably the same friends and family get asked for money or labour at various sausage sizzles and suburi-athons etc. This time, it was really nice to be able to offer them something back for their support. Even better, something relevant to kendo with the custom label and link to Japanese culture, and really good tea, too. A great fundraising tool that we will certainly be using again."—David Wong

So, why not ease the financial burden on your club or federation and partake in the samurai legacy at the same time? If you are cold, Samurai Green Tea will warm you. If you are too hot, it will cool you. If you are depressed, it will cheer you. If you are excited, it will calm you. Each cup of Samurai Green Tea represents an imaginary voyage. It is liquid wisdom with all of the health benefits Japanese green tea is famous for. Samurai Green Tea is the real deal.

Samurai Green Tea is

- **100%** PRODUCED IN JAPAN
- **100%** FREE OF PRESERVATIVES OR ADDITIVES
- **100%** ORIGINAL
- **100%** READY FOR DOJO FUNDRAISING
- **100%** PERSONALISED TO USE AS A QUALITY GIFT FOR ANY OCCASION
- **100%** DELICIOUS AND HEALTHY

Contact Graham, your tea and fundraising consultant, at **tea@kendo-world.com** to see how he can help you raise money for your federation or club.

contact us **tea@kendo-world.com**   about   **http://www.j-conceptsjapan.com/samurai-tea/**

J-Concepts 1082-1 Ieyama Kawane-cho, Shimada-shi, Shizuoka, 428-0104 JAPAN Tel.: +81 (0)80-3689-5978

Shinai Sagas

The Secret of My School

By Charlie Kondek
Artwork by Phillip Solomon

The disciple awoke, startled, sitting up against the wall, in the darkness outside the light of the dying fire, and found the master also awake. Such was his devotion that his first thought, upon waking, before he had even fully appreciated that he had fallen asleep leaning against the wall, was to ask the master's calm, half-submerged and bearded face, "Are you cold? I've let the fire die. Excuse me." And he rushed with limbs not yet roused to tasks to the woodpile, to add wood to the fire in the common hearth. The master was sitting with his arms folded into the sleeves of his jacket and wrapped around the sword that lay against his breast and shoulder, and now he moved, and in the suddenly leaping fire the smile beneath the lines of his moustache was visible.

"Did you fall asleep, too?" the master asked, not looking at the disciple or the fire. "Tell the truth. I was asleep. Were you?"

As usual, the disciple's tongue was stuck, the thoughts in his mind, the words not spoken, dashed against it, piled up there. "Sensei!" The word escaped in a whisper, for they were surrounded by other people sleeping at various distances from the fire's heat in the inn's common room. "Forgive me," said the disciple. "I intended to keep watch all night."

The master was still smiling, fainter now, and stroking the obsidian arrow of hair at his chin. "So did I," he said softly. "So did I." Rising, thrusting the sword into his *obi* and seeking his shoes with the toes of his stockinged feet, he added, "One shouldn't spend what might be his last night on earth sleeping. But I suppose" — he sought the doorway — "one shouldn't spend it drinking, either."

The master was gone, making water. But the disciple, though he too had to make water, would not move, as if he had not permission to do so, as if in punishment for some failing.

When the master returned he slipped the sword from his belt and leaned it against the wall within easy reach. He thrust his palms toward the fire, and extended his feet to it. "More *sake*, master?" the disciple asked. "Tea?"

"Are you having any?" the master asked. "I could do with tea. Maybe I should just go back to sleep. A fine party we had. Why not spend one's last night sleeping? Sleep, wake, what does it matter? I'm pretending there's a difference."

The disciple busied himself with tea, adding water to the leaves in the half-drunk pot and lowering it to the heat of the stove. "Sensei, how can you speak this way? Do you always feel like this, the night before a duel? That each one could be your last?" To the disciple, this seemed an appropriate ritual, even if unnecessary to a man of the master's power, a token gesture of humility and fatefulness by a man that was otherwise unable to be harmed, impervious to pain or death.

The master again smiled that ghostly, bearded smile, and jammed a thumb against the side of his head, as if crushing and wiping away an insect. He called the disciple by name. "S—, you've only followed me—against my will, I remind you—since O— village. There is much you don't know about me, and you've only seen me fight once. A spectacular fight, it's true, though a disgusting brawl in the street. But, I understand why you can't judge the significance of this night." He measured his next words. "I urged you not to follow me. I've taught you nothing at all—I have nothing to teach. Maybe tomorrow I'll teach you how to die."

Again, the disciple choked on thoughts, on words. They seemed to drop, unspoken, soundless, from his mouth. The teapot began to steam. "How many hours until dawn?" the master asked. "I do not know," the disciple stammered. "I haven't yet heard the striking of the hour. Maybe two hours? Three?"

The master folded his arms, lowered his chin to his chest, and tugged his ebon beard absently with thumb and forefinger.

The disciple had lost his way in the conversation and glanced around helplessly to find the way back to the subject. "Sensei, help me understand what you are saying. How is tomorrow's duel with T— different than any other? How—how can you say that you are not a great swordsman and that this foe will be the undoing of a long, successful career?"

The master was probing his face with his fingertips. "I can't decide if I'm still drunk or just dizzy and leaden with hangover," he said. "Maybe that's the way to do it. With a hangover. Certainly, it's an opinion I've heard expressed before by other schools."

He looked around him at the other pilgrims sharing the hearth, travellers all, seeking to defray expenses by spending the night in the common room, a cloth merchant here, two bookkeepers there. Then he noticed again the disciple's confused gaze, felt once again a patient pity for him. The disciple had a round, pumpkin-like head. His reverent, whiskerless mouth and eager, black eyes attended the master from behind a billowing curtain of flickering firelight and soft smoke. The master sighed and watched the teapot. "You know that I am a student of the —— school," he said. "My teacher was chosen as the successor by his teacher. Another in his school broke off to form a separate branch. My master was, is, a skilful teacher of the *ryū* he inherited, but many of his students, myself included, always wondered if he was indeed a skilful fighter. You see…" The master sought the face of the disciple to gauge his reaction. "Just because a person can teach doesn't mean he can do. Well, that's what we always wondered about my teacher, those of us with enough talent to see it. Yes, he was a brilliant teacher, technically very correct. But we always wondered if his greatest gifts were not as a swordsman but a… politician perhaps."

The tea was ready. The disciple chose two relatively clean cups and poured tea into them, served one to the master. The master said, "I don't know when I became conscious of the idea that I might be in some ways better than my teacher. But I think this suspicion plagued him, too. It was clear as I progressed in the school that he treated me differently, favouring other students for advancement. I think he was grateful when I announced my intention to undertake the path of a *shūgyōsha* and strike out on the road. It absolved him of the dilemma of having to choose between me and another student to inherit the *ryū*. Or of having me make a break, start another branch, which had embarrassed his master and would embarrass him. I left, and the school remained intact though, in my view, sheltered."

"Sheltered?"

"Yes. From the pressure of having to prove itself in actual combat. Just as many other *ryū* are likewise sheltered." The master tested his tea with his lips and eyed the disciple from beneath thoughtful black brows. "Since striking out on my own, experiencing the deadly freedom of personal combat, I have fought 11 duels and a handful of petty skirmishes like the one you witnessed. Tomorrow will be my twelfth duel. That's a very significant number, you know. It means a cycle is complete, that it is time for death and, if possible, rebirth.

"Well, how can I explain? Maybe I can really teach you something, T—. A real fight with swords is only a little bit like practice. I mean, you will fight as you trained, and so will the other fellow. But, things will happen that you never expected—accidents, or, it will be nothing like you imagined. Luck and chance play a part, too. And it's always shorter, or longer, than you anticipated.

"Eleven duels. I've been very lucky and maybe a little bit bold. When I fought H— of the —— school, I remember he favoured utilising distance, so I fought him very close and then surprised him in the attack by cutting even closer—he could have struck off my head if he'd adjusted. A— believed in attacking the appendages of an opponent, the hands and legs, so I kept my distance there and batted away his attacks until he ran out of ideas, then closed in—I have a scar on my arm from that one. G— believed in strength, so I tired him out. I— believed in speed, so I let that fight drag on. This may sound like strategy to you, and it is, but, how shall I put this—each of my opponents should have been able to adjust their methods to defeat my gambits. No swordsman is complete that doesn't adapt. The truth is, I have been very lucky, each time. I am only telling you the obvious. There were times when I succeeded for no reason at all."

The master paused to see if his words were having any effect on the disciple. The disciple, his face like a moon in the fire flickered darkness, seemed to be considering, but there was no obvious signal of comprehension. In fact, the disciple was struggling to understand the implications of the master's words while also trying to control the discomforting need to urinate. The master wasn't even sure what he was saying himself, so the ideas floated between them in the smoky darkness.

"What I mean is," the master concluded, "I have skill. My opponents have skill. I use strategy. They use strategy. If I have succeeded in surviving 11 of these duels, it is not because I am superior in swordsmanship but because, all things being equal, the results have just happened to favour me. But this opponent that I face tomorrow—today, rather—is superior. The tiny god of luck will not be enough to turn the match to my favour. He has bigger gods on his side. He has no need of luck."

"Then," the disciple stammered. "Sensei, are you expecting to…?"

The master sipped tea from beneath his moustache and said, "If you are waiting for me to dismiss you to use the toilet, please be dismissed. But while you're up, will you fetch my bag? There is ink, brush and paper there and I can compose my final ode."

The disciple hesitated. Though he had been given clear direction, he struggled with how to obey, which impulse to follow. In that moment, the warden struck the time and one of the bookkeepers that had been matching the master drink for drink came to life, mumbling, "Hey, *rōnin*, still awake? It's almost dawn. You'll be drunk for your duel!"

*****

In the heat of the afternoon, the master stood on the bridge and gazed down into the water, aware of, but indifferent to, the people that passed around him in their *kimono*, *obi*, sandals and *geta*. This indifference was in part enabled by the one good eye with which the master viewed the scene—hot air, shallow water rippling lazily over weedy stones; half his face and his other eye were shrouded in carefully wrapped bandages. A tendril of pink scar licked a corner of his beard.

The disciple approached. It was near the hour when the sun would begin to set, and enflame the west side of the town with long, low rays. "Sensei," said the disciple, bowing, pumpkin head perspiring, "I paid the surgeon's bill with the money you gave me. Tomorrow he will come to examine you again."

A serene smile played across the master's hedged lips. The one visible eye signalled amusement. "Did the surgeon say whether I'll have use of this eye again?"

"He told me nothing he hadn't already told you." The disciple stood and wrung his hands as the master leaned against the hot rail of the bridge. In one of the master's hands was a towel. In the other, paper.

"It seems I really have taught you nothing," the master said. "I was supposed to teach you how to die. I couldn't even manage that."

The disciple began to object, but the words would not come. He wanted to tell the master that he thought he'd learned enormously from the duel, but he lacked the ability to describe what he'd witnessed and absorbed. The psychic connection between the combatants as they'd taken the field. The tension wrought between them as they'd drawn, and taken stances, and moved —one forward a dusty step, the other back—and then the excruciating drama of stillness that ensued when each man had adjusted his *kamae*, maybe shifted a foot or a hip, then the pause, the observance, like dogs bearing fangs, til another step, another shift, the raising or lowering of the sword's point, provoked the other. How could the disciple describe the ordeal of waiting, the growing tautness of the connection between the two swordsmen, still no blow having been struck, the edging, edging forward, the retreat, and then the break of action like lightning from gathering cloud, the cut, the counter, the counter cut, the stalemate, the return, the anxious resetting of stance and quick adjustments to the position of foot and knee.

The disciple had language for this, he felt. If only he could find the words, he could have described how the duellists, exemplary specimens of their schools, had drawn the drum skin tighter between them through repeated sorties and then adjustments to stance, position and movement. And then the proprietary moves of the schools, after several passes, were exhausted, and now they came to more primeval blows—a wide cut to the shoulder, a dodge, a counter cut, broad, across the abdomen, absorbed, steel on steel, and now the blades in savage arcs over the head, ringing like temple bells, now they were cheek to cheek and using their bodies to push, a hand on a wrist, a backward slash…

The duel had been a linked poem. The disciple could almost note the stanzas, the shifts. Perhaps someday he would have words. Perhaps if he could not speak them, he could write them.

The master was speaking again. "Twelve duels. Time for a rebirth. If I never regain the use of this eye, a poor *shūgyōsha* I'll be. But I may yet be of use as an instructor somewhere. Tell me, any objection to settling down?"

"No—none," the disciple stammered.

"I'd hoped to be rid of you—I mean that affectionately, T—. But I must admit I'll need a caretaker til I recover from my wounds. I guess it's time to think about the future."

The disciple nodded, bowed. Yes, maybe he could capture on paper what he'd learned. The lowering sun cast rays beneath the bridge, in which boys played at splashing. "That document," the disciple said, gesturing to the master's hand. "Can I keep it for you?"

The master glanced at it with his one eye. "No," he answered. "It's wrong, now. It belongs to another time. I'll have to write new ones." And before the disciple could object, the master let it fall from his hand into the shallow water. "Come," said the master. "Let's watch the sun set on this era. What a brave man he was."

The water under the bridge was shallow at that time of year. The paper that fell settled on the stones. The current of the river tickled the paper, eventually penetrating it, carried it a few feet downstream, where it got stuck again. By then, the characters in the statement had been smeared, illegible, so that it could not be read. Slowly, the words, which had been composed the night before the duel, were obliterated.

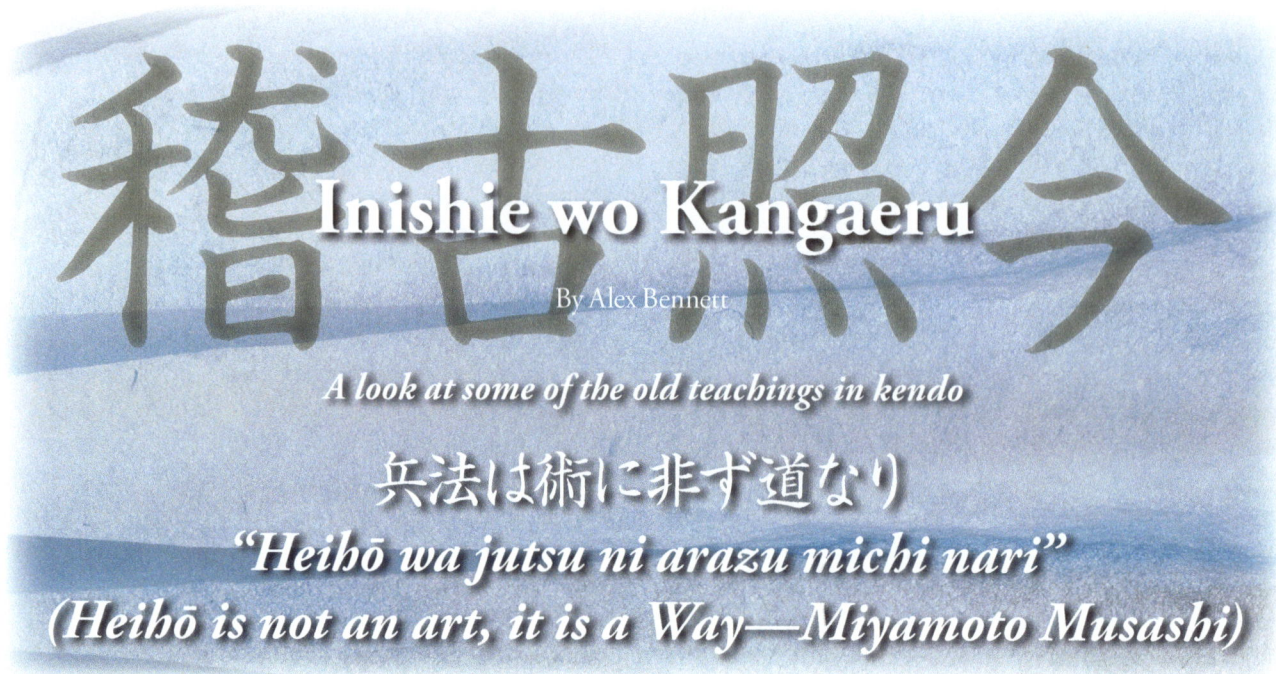

Inishie wo Kangaeru

By Alex Bennett

A look at some of the old teachings in kendo

兵法は術に非ず道なり
"Heihō wa jutsu ni arazu michi nari"
(Heihō is not an art, it is a Way—Miyamoto Musashi)

The word *heihō*, also known as *hyōhō*, originally meant the study of weapons and military science and strategy, but over time changed to mean martial arts in general, and later on swordsmanship in particular. Way (*michi*) in general terms refers to a way or ethos for living one's life, but also has a profoundly deep philosophical aspect. In the ancient Chinese Confucian text *Zhōng yōng* (Doctrine of the Mean), it is stated, "What Heaven confers is called 'nature'. Accordance with this nature is called the Way. Cultivating the Way is called 'education'."

Many great warriors over the centuries have drawn parallels between the trade of killing and universal principles of the Way. Miyamoto Musashi, for example, wrote in *Gorin-no-sho*, "The Way of strategy is the Way of nature. When you appreciate the power of nature, knowing the rhythm of any situation, you will be able to hit the enemy naturally and strike naturally. All this is the Way of the Void." This sentiment has had a significant impact on the way in which the philosophy and principles of modern budo have evolved to the present day. In other words, technical proficiency is important for obvious reasons, but Musashi asserted that seeking a higher plane of truth through the vehicle of the art was even more so.

Musashi was a seasoned warrior who had an existential appreciation of life and death. We 21st centuryites do not engage in mortal combat the way Musashi and his contemporaries did, but their wisdom gained from such a precarious existence is still very pertinent, and can be accessed through kendo and the other martial arts.

Great warriors such as Tsukahara Bokuden taught that the sword was not for killing others, but for cutting away the evil intent and avarice in one's own heart. This was the ultimate objective of the Way of the sword. Another giant of his day, Yagyū Tajima-no-Kami, wrote, "I have learned that swordsmanship is not to beat others, but instead to discipline the self." All of these statements point to the ideal that *heihō* is much more than just the science of slaughter. It also guides us to spiritual emancipation and offers us access to universal principles that pervade all pursuits. To quote Musashi again, "I studied morning and evening searching for the principle, and came to realise the Way of strategy when I was fifty. Since then I have lived without following any particular Way. Thus with the virtue of strategy I practise many arts and abilities—all things with no teacher."

To him, the fundamental principles he mastered

through the medium of swordsmanship were absolutely applicable to everything else he did in his life. Apart from being a peerless swordsman, he was also a highly acclaimed ink artist and carpenter, and approached these activities with the same clarity of mind and solemnity as he did in a fight to the death with swords. "Then you will come to think of things in a wide sense and, taking the void as the Way, you will see the Way as void."

How does this apply to the modern day kendoka? Many people think that the so-called "Way" of kendo simply implies self-cultivation in the moral and physical sense. In particular, training in the techniques of kendo, in accordance with the principles of the sword, tempers the body, strengthens the mind, and encourages a higher degree of respect for self and others. It does have the potential to make us better people, and this dimension is crucial in kendo culture. In spite of being fairly obvious, another dimension to the "Way" of kendo is often forgotten in the sometimes nebulous hype and moral imperative to "become a better person". That is, how can the principles of kendo be applied to other more mundane aspects of one's daily activities?

After 30 years of studying kendo, I often catch myself inadvertently looking for ways to apply kendo knowledge to all manner of situations. For example, driving a car has become an extension of my kendo. Distance, timing, pre-emption, physical reflexes, emotional control, avoiding *hansoku, enzan-no-metsuke, zanshin*… All of these skills and ideals that I have pondered and honed through my study of kendo are totally applicable when taking hold of the steering wheel.

I used to think, "If this was kendo, what would I do?" Now, I do not even pose the question. It is presumptuous to say that "everything I do now IS kendo", but it's getting closer. At least I can say that I am starting to understand what Musashi meant, and what a Way truly is. Kendo offers a unique paradigm for all human action. The wisdom of the ancients is a wonderful thing.

Miyamoto Musashi ; *Grapes and Squirrel*
Ink on paper ; 127 × 47cm

Hybrid Indigo Leather

極
KIWAMI

Japan Blue × Synthetic Leather
The pinnacle of craftsmanship

After many years of research, Tozando have succeeded in dyeing high performance synthetic leather using traditional genuine Indigo-dye

This pioneering technology will revolutionize the world of Kendo Bogu

"If it succeeds, it will be a miracle".
It was said that trying to dye synthetic leather using genuine Indigo-dye would be an impossible task. But the engineers at Tozando succeeded in creating the "Hybrid Indigo Leather", a new material that is completely different from the chemically-dyed synthetic leather that is widely used in the Bogu industry today.

The Indigo-dye is alive and the color and the vibrancy does not lose, even compared to genuine Indigo-dyed Deerskin.
The elegant Indigo-dye truly shines when applied on Kendo Bogu.

Hybrid Indigo Leather
Groundbreaking material Into a new era of Kendo Bogu

Light weight & durable the best material for Kendo Bogu

Compared to natural leather, Hybrid Indigo Leather is 50% lighter, and also more durable than current materials. This allows us to make lighter Bogu that are easier to move in, which in turn allows you to speed up your game and wear your Bogu for longer periods of time without getting your stamina drained by wearing heavy equipment.

Surpassing natural leather useful functions

We have incorporated cutting-edge technology also in the base material of the synthetic leather itself.
To counter unwanted odor, the Hybrid Indigo Leather has anti-bacterial properties, and is also very breathable, able to absorb and evaporate moisture much faster than natural leather. It is also thinner and lighter than Orizashi cotton, even though the durability is better than current materials at the same thickness. Truly the ultimate material for Bogu in every word and sense.

Unparalleled beauty even with regular use

The beautiful grid pattern that can be seen on high quality Hand-stitched Bogu will fade with time, however the pattern on a Bogu made with Hybrid Indigo Leather will not. This is since while the lines drawn on deerskin can be erased and re-done as needed, however, on the Hybrid Indigo Leather, it is close to permanent.
This puts the skill of the craftsman to the test, with no room for error, each Futon is skillfully crafted.

Strong against dye bleed & discoloration Keeping your equipment in it's optimal state

The technique of dyeing synthetic leather with Indigo-dye was perfected by Tozando. What makes it so special, is the beautiful and elegant color of genuine Indigo-dye. This color was previously not achievable on synthetic materials, but now the Indigo color of the Hybrid Indigo Leather is as brilliant or even more so than Deerskin, without dye bleed or discoloration, it will always keep the characteristic Indigo-dye color of your Bogu at it's optimal state.

Available soon, at www.tozandoshop.com